Editor's Picks

False Impressions

ACE BRYANN

A masterful blend of romance, political intrigue, and suspense, False Impressions showcases Ace's brilliance through twists, depth, and emotion.

Paperback: £15.43

https://bit.ly/43OBYQ0

Gigglet

A.M. BERKOWITZ

Heartwarming tale with vibrant illustrations, delightful characters, and valuable lessons on friendship, teamwork, and nature's joys. Perfect children's book!

Kindle: £6.53

https://bit.ly/4kufCJA

Gangster

BETTY BRANDT PASSICK

Masterfully crafted, Gangster in Our Midst combines rich historical detail, engaging characters, and Midwestern charm into an unforgettable narrative.

Paperback: £15.46

https://bit.ly/4kTsVDp

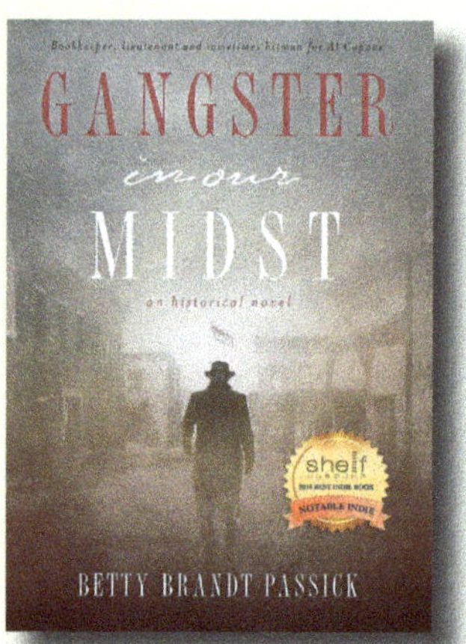

Change of Heart

CRISTINA LEPORT

"Change of Heart" is a riveting medical thriller, expertly blending suspense, crime, and medical intrigue. A must-read page-turner!"

– Margaret Earing,

Hardcover £21.99

https://amzn.to/3SjkhSb

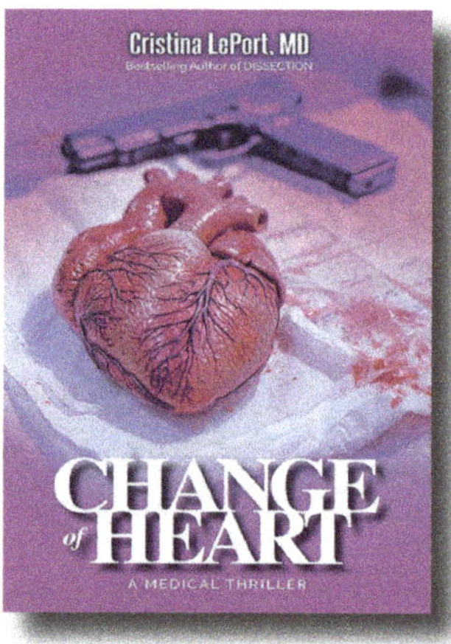

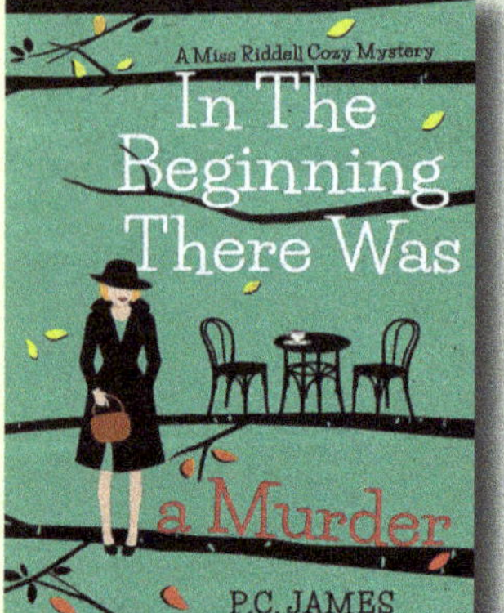

In The Beginning, There Was a Murder

P.C. JAMES

"In The Beginning, There Was a Murder" is a gripping cozy mystery with twists, smart heroine, and 1950s intrigue. Must-read!

Papperback: £9.99

https://amzn.to/3OgDaTr

The Dying Party

JEFF KELLAND

"The Dying Party explores a future where climate change is unstoppable, following both the poor and elite's survival struggles."

Kindle: £2.14

https://amzn.to/3CuFmE9

Words Whispered in Water

SANDY ROSENTHAL

"Words Whispered in Water" reveals Sandy Rosenthal's battle to uncover the truth behind Hurricane Katrina's levee failures, challenging powerful entities."

Paperback: £10.50

https://amzn.to/4fwsJqT

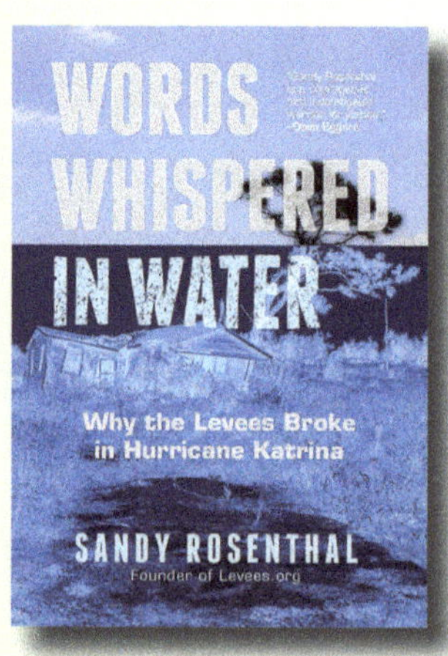

Midnight Marriage

LUCINDA BRANT

"Midnight Marriage" follows Julian's secret quest to win Deb's heart, set in the lavish Georgian aristocracy.

paperback: £9.99

https://amzn.to/3UUkbl6

Your Gateway to Endless Stories

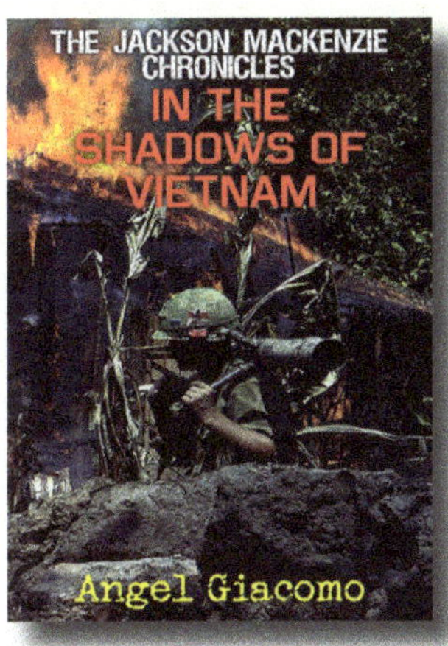

The Jackson MacKenzie Chronicles

ANGEL GIACOMO

"A gripping tale of courage and resilience", "In the Shadows of Vietnam" masterfully captures the Vietnam War's intense challenges.

– Steven Setil

Kindle: £2.95

https://amzn.to/40UZnxN

Immersed in West Africa

TERRY LISTER

"Immersed in West Africa" by Lister is a captivating exploration of diverse cultures, offering profound insights and inspiring connections through its vivid storytelling and adventurous spirit.

Paperback: £7.49

https://amzn.to/4hPOjbp

Fairy Tale Science

SARAH ALBEE

"*Fairy Tale Science* by Sarah Albee brilliantly blends fantasy and facts, making science enchanting and accessible for curious young minds."

Hardcover: £14.99

https://amzn.to/3Od7nTf

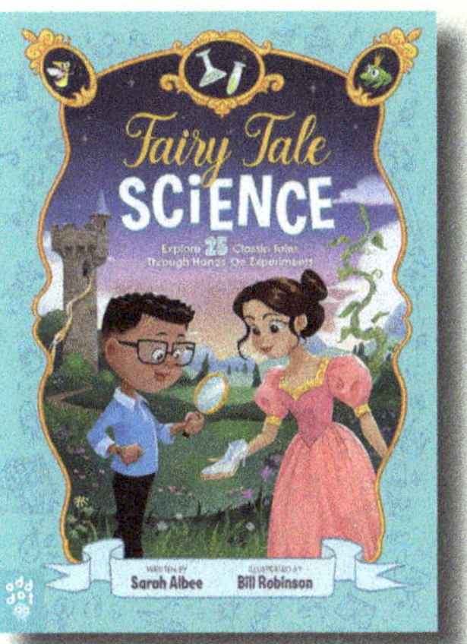

The Darkest Passages

LEN HANDELAND

"The Darkest Passages" captivates with its intense blend of passion, revenge, and supernatural intrigue, delivering a thrilling vampire saga.

Hardcove: £14.54

https://amzn.to/3UVUErW

Mushroom Cloud

THOMAS J. YEGGY

"Mushroom Cloud" masterfully blends historical fact with gripping fiction, offering a compelling narrative on nuclear disarmament's critical importance.

Paperback: £7.99

https://amzn.to/3YUALCJ

The Midnight Man

JULIE ANDERSON

"The Midnight Man" captivates with its atmospheric post-war London setting and clever mystery, featuring determined female sleuths.

Paperback: £10.99

https://amzn.to/3zTe4pF

Defiance Passage

TERRY OVERTON

"Defiance Passage" follows brave teens in a dystopian world, seeking freedom and knowledge while evading oppressive forces. Adventure awaits!

Paperback: £10.24

https://amzn.to/3ZazCrV

You Will Never Be Me

JESSE SUTANTO

"As an influencer's life unravels, jealousy and revenge take center stage in this suspenseful tale filled with unexpected twists and dark humor.

Paperback: £9.73

https://amzn.to/3O9UtFI

VOICES OF LITERATURE

What's INSIDE

AUTHOR INTERVIEWS

What's INSIDE

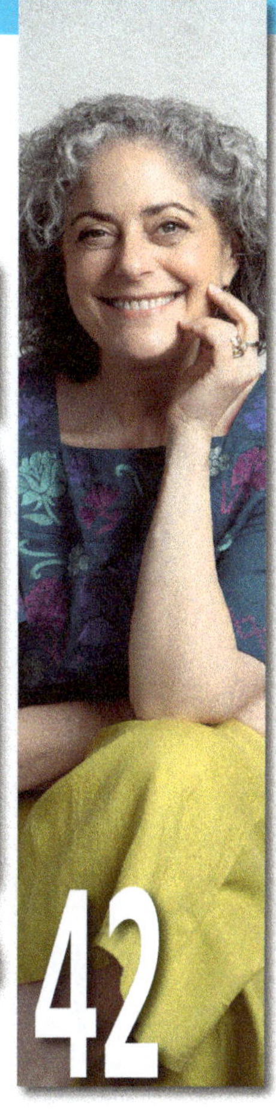

EDITOR'S CHOICE highlights exceptional books, offering insig… guide readers in discovering their next great read.

What's INSIDE

Issue 52 -2025

ART & MEDIA

Scan QR to read online or updated issue.

From the Editor

Welcome to the 51st issue of Reader's House, a celebration of literature, art, and the stories that connect us all. We are thrilled to feature the immensely talented Karen White on our cover as our Star Interview. With nearly two million books in print and a place on the New York Times bestseller list, Karen is not just a prolific author; she is a master storyteller who weaves her Southern roots into rich narratives that resonate with readers worldwide.

In our exclusive interview with Karen, we explore her journey from the business world to bestselling author, her creative process, and the profound experiences that inspire her writing. We delve into the heart of her novels, where complex characters and evocative settings come alive — from the vibrant streets of New Orleans to the historic charm of Charleston. Her upcoming release, *That Last Carolina Summer*, set to debut in July 2025, promises to add another gem to her remarkable oeuvre.

This issue is particularly special as we expand our horizons beyond literature. We are proud to showcase an array of exceptional authors, including Alan Lessik, Barbara Avon, Colleen Coyne, Debbie Cassidy, Eileen Harrison Sanchez, Eleanor D. Alspaugh, Hope Brooks, Jonathan Cox, Kate Church, Len Joy, Leonce Gaiter, M.J. Hollows, Marcy Bialeschki, Mark Anthony, Matt Barrows, Jessica Beebe, Ritu Hemnani, Susan Weis-Bohlen, Walter B. Curry Jr, whose unique voices contribute to the rich tapestry of contemporary literature. Each author brings a distinct perspective, and we are honored to provide a platform for their insights and inspirations.

Moreover, in collaboration with WowwArt magazine, we highlight interviews with today's most talented artists, celebrating the intrinsic connection between art, media, culture, and literature. At Reader's House, we believe that these realms are intertwined, and we are excited to explore how they shape our world. This partnership with WowwArt magazine allows us to bridge the narrative of literary artistry with the vibrant expressions found in visual and performing arts.

As we turn the pages of this issue, we invite you to immerse yourself in the stories and experiences of remarkable individuals — from bestselling authors to inspiring artists. Their words remind us of the power of storytelling and its ability to unite us across different mediums and backgrounds.

Thank you for your continued support of Reader's House. We hope this issue sparks joy, inspiration, and a deeper appreciation for the arts in all their forms.

PUBLISHER: READER'S HOUSE MAGAZINE, A Subsidiary of NewYox Media Group. 200 Suite 134-146 Curtain Road, EC2A 3AR London, United Kingdom t: +44 79 3847 8420
editor@readershouse.co.uk II http://readershouse.co.uk II http://newyox.media

Exploring Queer Narratives Through Time

Alan Lessik discusses his inspiration, creative process, and research for writing deeply resonant novels that interweave personal history, spirituality, and queer themes while preserving and celebrating LGBTQ+ stories across cultures and time.

ALAN LESSIK

WEAVES HISTORY, IDENTITY, AND SPIRITUALITY INTO UNFORGETTABLE STORIES

as told to Zosia Roberts

"Fiction has the power to illuminate lives left out of textbooks, the very lives that created history."

Alan Lessik is a literary force whose works transcend the boundaries of time, geography, and the human condition itself. A novelist, Zen practitioner, queer activist, and figure skater, he brings a unique alchemy of lived experience and meticulous research to his storytelling. His most recent novel, *Make the Dark Night Shine*, is a shining accomplishment, earning the Gold Medal from Literary Titan and the Silver Medal from the Global Book Awards. This remarkable work delves into themes of identity, history, and healing, skillfully intertwining personal narratives with the broader canvas of political and cultural shifts. Meanwhile, his debut novel, *The Troubleseeker*, shortlisted for the Publishing Triangle's prestigious Ferro-Grumley Award for LGBTQ Fiction, similarly weaves mythology, spirituality, and queerness in a heart-wrenching exploration of love and loss.

Lessik's devotion to authenticity is striking: he travels extensively to experience the places about which he writes, ensuring the historical and cultural accuracy of his settings. His ability to weave fact with fiction elevates his historical novels into immersive and poignant masterpieces. From tracing the echoes of Zen Buddhism in his work to deftly exploring Cuban and Greek mythologies, Alan's characters embody richly human experiences while never shying away from their queerness. His steadfast commitment to showcasing unashamed queer identities makes his novels essential contributions to LGBTQ+ literature, fostering visibility and celebrating the spectrum of life.

In this issue, we sat down with Alan to explore his vivid storytelling methods, his intersectional approach to research, and his insights into preserving LGBTQ+ history through literature. From the deeply personal inspirations for his narratives to his reflections on spirituality in his work, this conversation offers a window into the mind of a writer who is redefining the boundaries of historical fiction and queer storytelling. Alan Lessik's voice, both on and off the page, is one the literary world is fortunate to have.

What inspired you to weave your family history into Make the Dark Night Shine, and how did you balance fact with fiction?

My favorite aunt, Nina Friedberg Uchida never knew her father. On a visit when she as 91, she told me that her children had discovered that her father had traveled from Japan to NY where she had been living with her mother in the 1930s. With a gleam in her eyes, she said, "I know her was looking for me." For the first time in her life, she believed that her long-lost father loved her. Instantly, I had a vision of his story and why despite this journey he did not find his daughter.

I had very few facts to go on and like all family stories, we are counting on unreliable narrators for the details. Ultimately, through my research, the person she thought was her father likely was not. But this particular famous Japanese diplomat had his own rumored backstories that gave unexpected direction to the novel. So even though, he was not Nina's real father, I adapted what is known of his historical story to the novel. I spent a significant time researching the political, economic and social milieus of Japan, Constantinople, Paris and London from the early 1900's to 1941 when the story ends. To imbue a sensory feel of a place, I always travel to all of the places that appear in my novels. Walking through an old market, sitting in a café or Zen temple and watching people go by is a key ingredient to my success as a writer.

> Alan Lessik crafts extraordinary novels that beautifully blend historical depth, emotional resonance, and unapologetic queer representation with breathtaking storytelling.

How has your practice of Zen Buddhism influenced your writing style and the themes you explore in your novels?

For Make the Dark Night Shine, the diplomat that we first meet in the book, later becomes a Zen priest as he heals from his family traumas and begins to explore his own family history. I studied Japanese a bit and traveled through Zen sites in Japan and did a retreat in the Zen temple that is described in the novel. My experiences there gave intimate life to how Zen can help one to find awareness and fulfillment while still experiencing all of the problems of living...sickness, death, loss of meaning, and the search for the self. But the reader does not have to know anything about Zen to appreciate the book. At its heart, like Zen itself, the book is imbued with what we already know and experience.

The Troubleseeker incorporates elements of Greek mythology and Santería—what drew you to these spiritual traditions, and how do they connect to the story?

After my Cuban-born partner died, I was the only one that knew all of his stories. He faced seemingly insurmountable odds in his life and survived them until he took his own life. Without realizing it, my novel answered the question of why did he die. His mother in Cuba taught ancient Greek, Egyptian and Roman history and René was always interested in these subjects. As I began to write his odyssey from Cuba on a small shrimp boat that almost did not survive the dangerous strait between Cuba and Florida, I looked back at the original Odyssey story for some of the character names. This led to the Greek gods and mythology. I was struck by the similarities between the Greek and the Afro-Cuban Santería pantheons. With similar ideas about fate and the limited ability of humans to control their own fate, who better to answer the questions of life and death. After several edits, a new character who became the narrator entered the book, the Emperor Hadrian, who had his own back story of love and grieving with his lover Antinous.

As a Queer activist and writer, how do you see the role of literature in shaping and preserving LGBTQ+ history?

The musical Hamilton ends with the Finale, "Who Lives, Who Dies, Who Tells Your Story." Our view of history has always been shaped not by the specific events themselves, but by who records and who remembers. Queer people are certainly not the only ones that have been eliminated from history or seen its history distorted by others. In the US and Europe, mostly men have structured how we view (or most often do not view) the achievements and experiences of women, African-Americans, immigrants, working class people and other groups. In the last decades, our understanding of the past has changed as new voices and perspectives have worked to bring these voices back into the historical timeline.

Yet despite the control over "history" by academics, fiction has long had the power to illuminate other lives left out of textbooks, the very lives that created history. Novelists and short story writers tell and preserve queer stories with their ability to create vivid and memorable details of lives and the times better than any text book.

Our stories are important. We know that queer people have always existed in all societies. So as I write historical novels, I research how queer people might have lived within the times and places I am writing about. Often, I just find traces pieces of information, around which I can build characters and storylines.

Your novels span different cultures, time periods, and perspectives—how do you approach research to ensure historical and cultural accuracy?

As a historical novelist in this sense, I want to make sure that the periods of time that I write about are accurate. So I immerse myself in research to make sure all the details are correct. Several times, I had to rewrite sections and move timelines around so that the dates reflected the actual events. In an early draft, my characters were immersed in the social life of Paris in 1920-22. Josephine Baker, a symbol of the time was one person they met. In the final fact-checking, I discovered that Baker did not arrive in Paris until later. Goodbye Josephine and hello Isadora Duncan, who was there at the right time.

I never know in advance where the information I find will take me. A now obscure battle in 1905 in Mukden then part of Manchuria, suddenly popped up in the story of a old man that my main characters meet in Dubrovnik.

> Alan Lessik's *The Troubleseeker* masterfully intertwines mythology, history, and queer themes in a poignant tale set in Havana. Blending Greek mythology, Cuban Santería, and modern struggles, the novel explores identity, resilience, and love. Both imaginative and moving, it's a vibrant, unforgettable story that bridges the timeless and the contemporary.

What advice would you give to other authors who want to write stories that blend personal history, spirituality, and LGBTQ+ themes?

My interest is to write queer stories where the characters experience no shame about who they are. They have doubts, they face the problems of everyday life, but none of my characters are ashamed of being queer and live their lives fully, despite facing homophobia.

We need queer stories that illuminate our lives, that call attention to the unseen and reflect the full complexity of humanity.

The Unique Voice Behind Award-Winning Fiction

Barbara Avon discusses her Italian heritage, multi-genre exploration, writing process, and the emotional depth that defines her unforgettable stories. A celebrated author, she offers wisdom for aspiring writers and storytelling enthusiasts.

BARBARA AVON

WEAVES MAGIC THROUGH WORDS AND GENRES

"One may never have the same ground beneath their feet, but the soil will forever be trapped within them."

as told to Dan Peters

Barbara Avon is a literary force to be reckoned with. A masterful multi-genre author, she has crafted spellbinding stories that span romance, horror, time travel, and paranormal fiction, earning her accolades and admiration from readers and literary circles alike. Her talent for infusing vivid, cinematic imagery into her writing, coupled with her ability to explore the deepest corners of the human condition, sets her apart as a storyteller. Whether it's the hauntingly beautiful "Revived," crowned as the "Horror Book of the Year" in 2022, or her recent triumph, the award-winning "Sultry Is the Night," Barbara Avon's works are a testament to her boundless creativity and passion for the written word.

Her Italian heritage breathes life into her narratives, adding rich cultural tapestries and personal authenticity to her characters and settings. With a style that is as versatile as it is distinct, Barbara has captivated readers with tales that transport them through time, stir their emotions, and leave them utterly spellbound. As she continues to push the boundaries of storytelling, her philosophy of writing from the heart resonates deeply—cementing her legacy as an author who truly believes in the magic of books, the magic of words, and the magic of love.

It is with great pride and enthusiasm that we present this insightful interview with Barbara Avon in this issue of *Reader's House*. Prepare to step into her world and uncover the inspiration behind her remarkable works, the craft of her writing process, and the unending devotion that fuels her literary journey. For those who have yet to discover her brilliance, there's no better time to be swept away by her universe of imagination.

How did your Italian heritage influence the themes and characters in your novels, particularly in your early works?

One may never have the same ground beneath their feet, but the soil will forever be trapped within them. I immigrated to Canada in 1974, but I will forever be Italian. My first female protagonist is Italian. (All of my primary protagonists are male, save for my latest horror story featuring Coralie.) One of my characters states, "Italians don't bleed blood. They bleed wine." He is referring to the Italian culture that revolves around food, drink, and family. My heritage is extremely important to me, and I fictitiously immortalize my own memories in my novels.

What inspired you to transition from writing romance with suspense elements to exploring genres like horror and paranormal romance?

I have always considered myself a storyteller. Picture a grandmother figure in a rocking chair with children encircling her as they sit on the floor, and she asks them, "What type of story would you like to hear today?" I wish to explore every aspect of life – whether romantic, disturbing, or hauntingly beautiful.

> Barbara Avon's evocative prose elevates storytelling. Her ability to transcend genres while maintaining an authentic voice is truly extraordinary.

Can you discuss the creative process behind your time travel stories and how you ensure historical accuracy within fictional narratives?

Google is a writer's best friend. One of my time travel stories, "Timepiece", opens in 1932, and it did take a lot of research to ensure historical accuracy regarding language, fashion, and way of life. The rest was inspired by all the classic movies I love that star iconic actors like Cary Grant, and Katharine Hepburn. Everything else came from my imagination. Science doesn't play a role in my time travel stories. The reader must suspend belief and simply enjoy being whisked away to a different era.

In your horror novels, such as "Revived," how do you balance psychological depth with supernatural elements to create compelling narratives?

Reality can often be scarier than fiction. I delve into the human psyche to dig out that which most scares us and has scarred us. Throw in a few ghosts, some ghastly scenes, and a deep sense of foreboding, and I end up with psychological horror such as "The Sixth Sense" rather than a bloody story like "Friday the 13th." Horror is one of my favourite genres to write and I always include a sub-love story. Love is a part of life, and therefore, it's also a part of death.

Your readers often describe your books as cinematic. How do you craft your stories to evoke vivid, movie-like imagery?

Words. It's a simple answer, but the most accurate one. A writer doesn't require a million words to paint a scene. A writer only needs the right words. It's the same reason my stories are typically short. With the perfect alphabetical palette, you can fill a page like a painter would a small canvas and still pack an emotional punch.

With "The Gift," you delve into the mystery genre. What challenges did you face in blending romance with suspenseful storytelling?

A budding, romantic relationship is suspenseful. It wasn't difficult to marry a romantic storyline with the mystery/thriller aspect. Michael Rossi, our male protagonist in "The Gift" and its sequel "Michael's Choice", is a stubborn, passionate, Italian who loves deeply. When the woman he loves puts herself in a dangerous, precarious situation, the reader finds themselves sharing his angst. One reader honoured me by reaching out to me to share their enthusiasm about the story. They stated that they were "unable to rest until Michael did". We are all flawed, and I think that readers appreciate characters that aren't cardboard cut-outs, but someone they can relate to, cheer for, or even mourn with.

What advice would you offer to aspiring authors aiming to successfully transition between different genres while maintaining a unique voice?

I've been told many times that my books are easily recognizable as Barbara Avon novels. That statement made me think, because I don't only write various genres, I write in various styles. Then I remember that little old grandma in the rocking chair who is holding her audience captive with her funny character voices, hand gestures, and charming intonation. Every author has a unique voice, just like grandma. I'd tell aspiring authors: Write without fear, write from your heart, and readers will remember you. However, just like a painter discards an uninspired canvas, don't be afraid to begin again. I, for one, am not adept at slaying dragons… then again, I have yet to try.

Barbara Avon's *Sultry, Is the Night* is a haunting, lyrical tale blending grief, love, and redemption. Set in a gritty 1980s city, it follows Mario's emotional journey after his mother's death. With evocative prose, raw honesty, and vivid imagery, the novel explores human struggles, self-discovery, and the healing power of love.

“The true account of Belgium's King Leopold II is more astonishing than fiction.”

Exploring Loss, Legacy, and Human Complexity in Literature

Colleen Coyne masterfully blends history, suspense, and deep emotional insight in her novels The Unintended Heiress and Bewept, sharing her inspirations, research process, and reflections on writing complex, character-driven fiction.

COLLEEN COYNE

COLLEEN COYNE BRINGS HISTORY AND EMOTION TO LIFE THROUGH COMPELLING STORYTELLING

as told to Z. Roberts

Colleen Coyne is an author whose literary prowess has captivated readers and critics alike, establishing her as a remarkable voice in contemporary fiction. With a keen ability to intertwine history, suspense, and profound human emotions, she crafts narratives that resonate deeply with audiences. Her debut novel, *The Unintended Heiress*, has garnered widespread acclaim, earning the Firebird Book Award in Fiction (First Time Published) and securing a place as a finalist in the prestigious Goethe Book Award, the American Fiction Award, and the Storytrade Book Awards. Her ability to weave intricate historical narratives into compelling fiction is further demonstrated in her second novel, *Bewept*, a deeply moving exploration of grief and memory. This work has been recognised in the National Excellence in Storytelling Contest, awarded the International Book Impact Award, and won the Storytrade Book Awards' Suspense/Thriller category.

Coyne's background in science lends a unique precision to her writing, allowing her to construct historically rich worlds while seamlessly integrating compelling character arcs. Her fascination with history and human psychology shines through in her narratives as she deftly explores the moral complexities of power, loss, and personal transformation. In *The Unintended Heiress*, she delves into the enigmatic reign of Belgium's King Leopold II, skilfully threading together past and present through a dual timeline that illuminates the far-reaching consequences of colonial exploitation. Meanwhile, *Bewept* offers an intimate and haunting portrayal of a woman's descent into grief, inspired in part by the author's personal observations of dementia and loss.

With a life spanning continents—Mystic, Connecticut, Roskilde, Denmark, and Villefranche-sur-Mer, France—Coyne brings a global perspective to her storytelling. Her experiences and extensive travels enrich her narratives, offering readers a vivid sense of place and emotional depth. Whether unearthing hidden histories or navigating the intricate landscapes of human emotion, her work reflects a profound dedication to both historical accuracy and literary artistry.

In this exclusive interview, Coyne provides insight into her inspirations, creative process, and the challenges of writing complex fiction. From the meticulous research behind *The Unintended Heiress* to the deeply personal influences that shaped *Bewept*, she shares her journey as an author, offering invaluable wisdom to aspiring writers.

What inspired you to write "The Unintended Heiress" and delve into the historical context of King Leopold II's reign?

We have a flat in Villefranche-sur-Mer,

> Coyne's literary brilliance shines through her historical depth, emotional complexity, and masterful storytelling, making her an exceptional voice in contemporary fiction.

France. Belgium's King Leopold II spent a lot of time in this area. From our balcony, we can see a few of his former properties. These magnificent villas sparked my curiosity about how a Belgian king could invest so much time and resources in another country. As I delved into research, I uncovered a fascinating narrative. The true account of Belgium's King Leopold II is more astonishing than fiction, encompassing his controversial reign, his young mistress, her longstanding lover, the King's three scandalous daughters, and the enigma of a disappearing fortune.

How did you approach the dual timeline structure in "The Unintended Heiress" to ensure a seamless narrative?

The original manuscript did not feature a dual timeline. However, this approach failed to sufficiently address King Leopold's exploitation of the Congolese people, which was the source of his wealth. Ignoring the suffering he caused for his personal gain would have been inappropriate and unjust. Utilizing a dual timeline allowed for an in-depth examination of the harsh measures he employed to fulfill his greed, providing balance to the narrative.

What was the most challenging aspect of writing "Bewept," particularly in portraying Anna's journey through grief and memory?

The inspiration for writing "Bewept" originated from observing my mother's descent into dementia and her grieving process following the loss of my father several decades earlier. I saw parallels in the stages of both her experiences. This observation led me to consider how susceptible individuals might be to manipulation while navigating either of these challenging journeys. "Bewept" was written during the pandemic. The prolonged isolation over many months made it difficult to avoid feelings of disconnection, akin to the experiences of the story's protagonist. There were times when I felt as though I were her.

How do you balance historical accuracy with creative storytelling in your novels?

My writing process is driven by a deep interest in understanding the reasons and mechanisms behind various phenomena, a passion that likely stems from my initial career as a scientist. Factual accuracy is a cornerstone of my work, providing a solid foundation for developing narratives. By incorporating historical settings, I can strike a balance between accuracy and creative storytelling, giving me more freedom to develop characters and stories within an already defined setting.

What role does setting play in your stories, and how do your personal experiences in Mystic, Denmark, and France influence your writing?

The French Riviera setting was important in my debut novel, "The Unintended Heiress." However, other than snowy and rural isolation, the actual setting was purposely less prominent in my second novel, "Bewept," or my current work in progress. The two later works focus more on a character's internal setting—their unique interior lives and experiences. My personal experiences living in Mystic, Denmark, and France and extensive global travel during my career have shown me how similar people everywhere are. Despite differences in food, language, clothing, and politics, people everywhere value family, friends, security, and home life.

What advice would you give to aspiring authors who want to explore complex themes like grief, history, and suspense in their work?

I have extensive experience in formal business and marketing writing. Transitioning to fiction was a new challenge, and I didn't know how or where to begin. The biggest challenge was learning to let go of the structured, fact-based approach of business writing and embrace the freedom and creativity of fiction. To get started, I took writing classes and attended writers' conferences. I advise aspiring authors to research both the craft and the business aspects of writing. After that, start writing and keep writing. Every author has their own

> Colleen Coyne masterfully explores grief, memory, and psychological suspense in 'Bewept'. Anna's journey through loss is both heart-wrenching and gripping, as past and present collide in a haunting mystery. With lyrical prose and emotional depth, Coyne crafts an unforgettable tale of resilience, trauma, and the courage to confront buried truths.

approach; some use rigorous outlining before writing, while others combine planning with spontaneous writing. After introducing the story, I develop characters by considering their motivations, fears, and actions in achieving their goals. At some point, the characters take over the work, leading to unexpected turns as the story progresses. Frequently, the midpoint of my narrative evolves in an unforeseen direction. This unpredictability is what I find most enjoyable about the writing process.

How do you hope your success and experiences as an author will inspire and guide other writers in their creative journeys?

My journey as an author has shown me that the writing community is a place of exceptional generosity, where knowledge and support are freely shared. Regardless of their level of success, most writers are eager to learn more about the craft and other writers' journeys. Writing can be a solitary journey, but the sense of community and camaraderie is truly inspiring. I hope to inspire others and be a part of this supportive community.

Strong Heroines, Mythical Worlds, And Heart-Stopping Stories

Deviyanee Cassidy discusses her creative process, love for mythology, strong heroines, and the evolution of her storytelling, offering insights and advice for aspiring authors in the fantasy romance genre.

Writing reverse harem was never planned. The characters demanded it, and so did the story. I was powerless to resist."

DEBBIE CASSIDY WEAVES MAGIC, MYTHOLOGY, AND ROMANCE INTO UNFORGETTABLE FANTASY WORLDS

as told to Ben Alan

Deviyanee Cassidy, known to her readers as Debbie Cassidy, is a literary force to be reckoned with. A USA Today Bestselling Author, she has carved a niche for herself in the realms of paranormal and urban fantasy, captivating audiences with her vivid imagination and masterful storytelling. Born in the UK and raised in a quaint town, Deviyanee's journey from a psychology graduate to a full-time author is as inspiring as the heroines she brings to life. Her works are a testament to her ability to weave intricate plots, create immersive worlds, and craft characters that linger in the hearts of readers long after the final page.

Drawing from her cultural heritage and a deep appreciation for Indian mythology, Deviyanee's stories are a rich tapestry of magic, danger, and romance. Her books, brimming with action and emotional depth, feature strong, take-charge heroines who navigate supernatural worlds with courage and wit. Whether it's the morally grey Anamaya from her upcoming romantasy Wicked Onyx or the unforgettable Quinn from her Wolves of Hawthorne Cove series, Deviyanee's characters are as complex and compelling as the worlds they inhabit.

In this exclusive interview, Deviyanee shares insights into her creative process, her love for mythology, and the organic evolution of her storytelling. She also offers invaluable advice to aspiring authors and gives us a glimpse into the

> Debbie Cassidy's 'Deadside Reapers Box Set 1-3' is a thrilling urban fantasy masterpiece. With a unique world, sharp humour, and captivating characters, it's impossible to put down. The blend of reapers, ghosts, and Necro city is brilliantly imaginative. A must-read for fans of action-packed, paranormal adventures with a touch of sass!

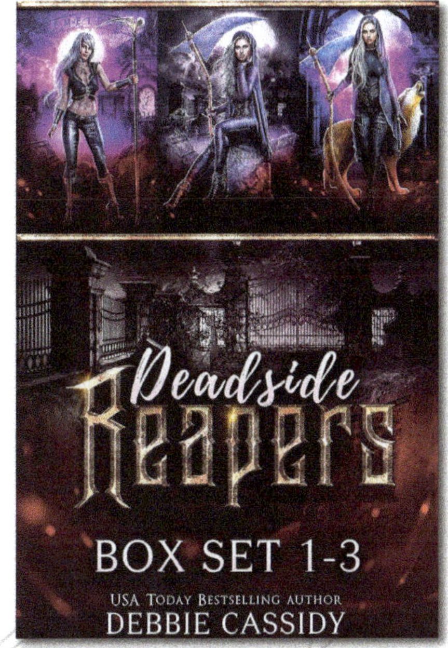

> Deviyanee Cassidy is a masterful storyteller, blending vivid world-building, compelling characters, and emotional depth into unforgettable fantasy adventures.

inspirations behind her beloved works. It's a privilege to delve into the mind of an author who continues to redefine the fantasy romance genre with every book she writes.

What inspired you to write in the urban fantasy and reverse harem genres?

I grew up reading urban fantasy books, and so it felt natural to write in that genre because I had such love for it. Writing reverse harem was never planned. It happened organically in my Chronicles of Midnight series. The characters demanded it, and so did the story. I was powerless to resist. I went with and loved it. More stories found me after that.

You're known for writing strong, take-charge heroines. Tell us a little about the heroine of your upcoming Romantasy Wicked Onyx?

Anamaya is one of my first morally grey heroines. She's last of a disgraced sorcerer bloodline. Exiled and cursed, Anamaya has had it tough. She's learned to rely solely on herself, and friendship might as well be a curse word in her book. When she discovers that her bloodline may not be guilty of the crime that they were punished for, she sets out to uncover the truth and get a little vengeance. Her journey takes her to Nightsbridge Academy, a place teaming with monstrous beings called horrors, and home to some of the most lethal supernal bloodlines.

I've had a blast writing Anamaya. She's witty, smart and knows how to fend for herself. I'm so excited for readers to meet her.

Can you share your creative process for building the unique worlds in your books?

I don't have a specific process. My worlds tend to come to me in dreams or bolts of inspiration. I then spend days and weeks thinking about them and making random notes on my phone until it's time to write the books. At this point I usually spend a day or two typing up my random notes and filling out the details. For me, the world building continues throughout my work on any series as I often discover new aspects of the world that I didn't know about to start with.

How do you balance action, romance, and character development in your novels?

I go with my gut. I can usually feel when something it off and figure out what is needed to fix the issue. I also have an amazing team of alpha and beta readers who aren't afraid to give me constructive criticism.

Are there any particular myths or legends that influence your storytelling?

So many! Where to start? You should see the reference section of my home library. I do a lot of reading on all kind of mythology. Norse, Celtic, Slavic, Greek, Hindu, I have it all. I often find myself going down rabbit holes filled with juicy information that spark ideas and stories. I like to put my own spin on things and go from there. Right now, I'm deep into Hindu mythology.

What advice would you give to aspiring authors in the fantasy romance genre?

If you plan on writing Fantasy Romance, then makes sure that you're familiar with the genre. Read the bestsellers so you can see why they are so loved. Read books on mythology to get your brain teaming with ideas. You can also do a deep dive on the internet where you'll find blogs on various mythology topics. I would also highly recommend reading some contemporary and paranormal romance books. Once again find the bestsellers. You'll learn how to write a gripping, emotive dynamic between characters. And finally, read a few popular fantasy books, so you can be inspired by the wonderful worldbuilding. Research is key!

Which of your characters do you feel most connected to, and why?

There's a little piece of me in each of my characters. Yep, even the villains. But if I had to choose, I would say, I was the most connected to Quinn, from my Wolves of Hawthorne Cove Series. I put way too much of myself into her, flaws included.

A Voice from the Past

Eileen Harrison Sanchez discusses her novel Freedom Lessons, exploring historical accuracy, diverse perspectives, and the on-going relevance of school integration, while sharing insights into her writing process and future projects.

EILEEN HARRISON SANCHEZ

A CONVERSATION ON HISTORY, IDENTITY, AND RESILIENCE

Eileen Harrison Sanchez, author of Freedom Lessons, shares her journey from educator to novelist, capturing pivotal moments in American history.

Eileen Harrison Sanchez is a remarkable storyteller whose debut novel, *Freedom Lessons*, has captivated readers with its poignant exploration of a pivotal moment in American history. A retired educator with a passion for reading and writing, Eileen brings a unique perspective to her work, drawing from her own experiences teaching in Louisiana during the late 1960s. Her dedication to capturing the complexities of that era is evident in her meticulous research and the authentic voices she brings to life in her characters. Eileen's commitment to storytelling is matched only by her love for family, friends, and the simple joys of life, such as traveling and bird watching from her gazebo. Her no-age mindset and perennial spirit shine through in her writing, inspiring readers to reflect on themes of identity, change, and resilience.

In this interview, Eileen shares insights into the creative process behind *Freedom Lessons*, discussing the challenges of balancing factual accuracy with the demands of fiction and the importance of presenting diverse perspectives. She reflects on the enduring relevance of school integration and the parallels between the struggles of the 1960s and today's ongoing discussions around race and education. Eileen also offers a glimpse into her involvement in writers' communities and how these connections have influenced her work. As she embarks on new writing projects, Eileen's passion for storytelling and her commitment to exploring meaningful themes continue to resonate with readers, ensuring her voice remains a vital part of the literary landscape.

Freedom Lessons is a powerful and heartfelt novel that vividly captures the complexities of school integration, exploring themes of race, identity, and resilience through compelling, diverse characters in 1969 Louisiana.

Freedom Lessons is based on your own experiences teaching in Louisiana during the late 1960s. What inspired you to transform those memories into a novel, and how did you balance factual accuracy with the creative demands of fiction?

The November 5, 1969, overnight closure of the segregated Black school I taught in was directly related to the little known Supreme Court Decision of Alexander v Holmes on October 29, 1969. Schools across the county were ordered to comply with the 1954 Brown v Board of Education decision to desegregate with "all deliberate speed". In many Louisiana towns, the year 1969 is known as The Crossover.

> Eileen Harrison Sanchez masterfully intertwines history and fiction, offering readers a profound exploration of identity, resilience, and social change.

A friend helped me to see that I witnessed a significant historical moment. I felt a responsibility to share it. The story was forty years old when I started to write it as a memoir. Memory fades and important facts required significant research and study of Black history. National and local newspaper articles, three doctoral dissertations, personal interviews, and a research visit to the reopened school provided the factual accuracy.

It was important to add points of view, develop characters, and scenes to tell the complete story. That required creative freedom to retell fictionalized events from my experience intertwined with researched experiences of Black high school students and Black teachers.

The novel presents the perspectives of three very different characters—Colleen, Frank, and Evelyn. How did you approach writing from such diverse viewpoints, and what were the challenges of capturing the authentic voices of each character?

My life experiences have proven to me that we are more alike than different. I focused on the importance of family and how family provides security, identity, and values. The characters of Colleen, Frank and Evelyn came from families that expected them to follow their moral compass. Of course, the biggest challenge was that two of the characters were Black and I am not. The voices of the Black characters came from a tremendous amount of research and challenged me to write in the voice of "other". Two Black authors read and edited the story. They felt that I captured the Black perspective fairly.

School integration is a central theme in Freedom Lessons. Given the current discussions around race and education in the U.S., what parallels do you see between the challenges faced in the 1960s and those we are encountering today?

The Supreme Court decision on Brown v BOE determined that separate schools for Black and white students was unconstitutional. The 1964 Civil Rights Act allowed the federal government to enforce desegregation. The states had until 1969 to comply with the mandate or lose federal funds. More than fifty years later our country has made changes and progress but there are still public schools that operate as segregated schools. Laws are necessary to protect our civil rights, but laws don't change people's opinions. People do, I can, I have. We must move forward.

As a member of various writers' communities and groups, how has your involvement in these communities influenced your writing process, especially when tackling complex historical and social issues?

Writing Freedom Lessons gave me a voice I didn't have as a young teacher. My writing communities, speaking events, and several awards gave me the support and confidence that my words will find readers. Freedom Lessons is being used as required reading for the final class of teacher training in a local university. Today's teachers have the benefits of training in social justice issues and responsible instructional practices to insure equality in education.

You describe yourself as a perennial with a no-age mindset. How has this outlook influenced your writing and storytelling, particularly in addressing themes of identity, change, and resilience in Freedom Lessons?

You are never too old to try something new. I'm a debut author in my seventh decade and I have expanded from one writing group to a vast community of authors and readers. My works-in-progress include my husband's coming of age story as a thirteen year old Cuban refugee granted asylum in the US. I don't have to look far to find inspiring stories of identity, change and resilience. Publication ensures the longevity of my voice.

In addition to writing, you enjoy traveling and bird watching. How do these activities contribute to your creative process, and do they provide any inspiration for your characters, settings, or narratives?

A recent trip to France inspired six essays ready for edits. A trip to Ireland will help me to write a family story of emigration to the United States. Imitating Monet, nature, flowers and birds at the feeders relax and inspire me. A yellow finch on a sunflower in my garden is my current painting project. You, dear reader, are reading my words, we are connected. Namaste.

A Soldier's Story, A Daughter's Perspective

Eleanor D. Alspaugh discusses weaving personal stories with historical research, the inspiration behind her award-winning books, and her passion for telling meaningful, heartfelt tales that transcend time and place.

ELEANOR D. ALSPAUGH

SHARES THE HEARTFELT STORIES BEHIND HER BOOKS AND THE LEGACY OF LOVE AND RESILIENCE

as told to Dan Peters

"My writing comes from my heart...sharing humanity in the challenges of life."

Eleanor D. Alspaugh is a name that beautifully resonates among lovers of heartfelt storytelling and true-to-life narratives. A multi-award-winning author, Eleanor masterfully weaves together deeply personal experiences with broader, universal themes, allowing readers to step into histories and lives that feel both intimate and pivotal. With a talent for unearthing profound lessons amidst the everyday, Eleanor's books—ranging from her laugh-out-loud insights into motherhood in *The Mommy-Go-Round*, to her poignant homage to military families in *When D is For Deployed*, to the richly detailed historical tapestry of *The Heart of a Soldier*—leave an indelible imprint on her audience.

In her latest triumph, *The Heart of a Soldier*, Eleanor achieves a remarkable feat: blending her father's personal wartime letters with meticulously researched historical context. Set against the backdrop of World War II, the book offers a window into the life of a soldier navigating love, duty, and danger, while simultaneously unfolding the human stories of those on the home front. The book has already garnered acclaim, including the 2023 Maincrest Media Book Award for Historical Non-Fiction and a Runner-up position in the 2024 Book Excellence Awards' Military Category—testaments to its brilliance.

Eleanor's work effortlessly embodies a balance between historical accuracy and emotional depth, reminding readers that history is not just about events, but about people: their love, sacrifices, and enduring humanity. Throughout her literary journey, she has maintained a strong connection to her roots as a proud wife, mother, grandmother, and storyteller, drawing inspiration from the lives of those closest to her.

In this exclusive interview, Eleanor takes us behind the scenes of her creative process, her inspiration for *The Heart of a Soldier*, and the legacy she hopes to leave through her writing. Whether you're drawn to history, personal reflection, or simply the honest truths of life, Eleanor D. Alspaugh's words promise to engage and inspire you deeply.

What inspired you to write "The Heart of a Soldier," and how did you approach combining personal letters with historical research?

Having saved my father's letters written home during World War II, my mother had often asked me to read the letters. I preferred just enjoying our visits and reminiscing of times when my father was still with us. However, once they were both gone, the letters became a lifeline to me, a way to reconnect with both my parents. As I read them, I felt moved by their story, and wanted to share the letters with others, particularly my family. Knowing how busy the world we live in is, I truly doubted that even my own family would find the time to open each envelope, see the personal notes tucked inside and read the letters filled with his experiences and heart. I also could not help but wonder what was going on in the world around them as they corresponded. It was then that I began to envision a book that included Dad's letters and some from my uncles, but also the history occurring as they wrote their letters. I felt others might enjoy the letters and learning about this historic time that my parents and so many others had lived through, presented in a personal manner rather than an impersonal history textbook. The book shares their story and at times, my thoughts as I entwined the letters with extensive research of significant World War II events and circumstances, in addition to sharing the combat path of my father's unit, the Sixth Armored Division of General Patton's Third Army.

> Eleanor D. Alspaugh captivates readers with heartfelt storytelling, fusing historical insight and emotional depth into timeless, inspiring narratives of love and resilience.

How did your father's letters influence your understanding of his experiences during World War II and his relationship with your mother?

My father's letters shared the perspective of a wartime soldier, determined to do his duty, yet realizing he might never return to her. Although deeply in love, he was selfless, loving my mother enough to encourage her to keep living life, having fun, even dating. Dad stated that he would not marry her before leaving for the war as he did not want her to have to spend her life caring for him if he returned severely injured.

What challenges did you face while researching and writing about the historical context of your father's service in the "Super Sixth"?

As I started writing The Heart of a Soldier, I faced numerous challenges. I was a working wife and mother, raising three children, and had achieved my desired position as an Assistant Vice President, with an abundance of responsibilities and writing assignments that accompanied that title. I was also secretly working on my first book, writing nights, weekends, and vacations, what would eventually be my first award-winning book, entitled The Mommy-Go-Round. Oh yes, and there was one more 'little hitch' to my plan for this book. I was a business major and as far from a historian as one could get. I had to face facts and postpone further writing or research until about 15 years later, when I grabbed at the opportunity of an early retirement. My dream of writing this book was still in my heart.

How do you balance writing about deeply personal family stories with ensuring historical accuracy and broader appeal?

My writing comes from my heart. My first very personal book shared a naïve working mother's initiation into motherhood. It was fun, sometimes challenging and perhaps, in lieu of therapy, I worked through my thoughts, feelings and observations as I wrote that first book. I later wrote a second book, When D is For Deployed, again heart driven as I watched my son-in-law deployed, and his wife, my daughter, and their young daughter try to continue their everyday life yet stay close to him, despite being worlds apart. As for The Heart of a Soldier, I was always aware of my father's heroism and the medals he received for his service, but that was family history. When finally reading his letters and immersing myself in World War II history, my heart was touched as I was transcended in time, touched by my parents' love at its beginning, and began to see the challenges and struggles they endured at home and away as he fought in this war. Together, it all gave me a much better understanding of the impact on their lives, their hopes and dreams and I realized that so many other lives were also put on hold as they faced similar challenges at home and around the world.

What message or lessons do you hope readers take away from "The Heart of a Soldier"?

Everyday life is known to have stress and challenges. As I researched and wrote this book, I read so much of the various challenges, dangers and difficult circumstances soldiers and citizens faced during World War II. As a result, I tried to draw readers into their long-ago reality. I encouraged people to imagine what their lives would be like if subjected to those same prejudices and struggles, not to mention the danger faced in battle or even extensive training. I do hope that readers of The Heart of a Soldier will better understand the hardships people endured during World War II and the lasting love of family that helped soldiers survive.

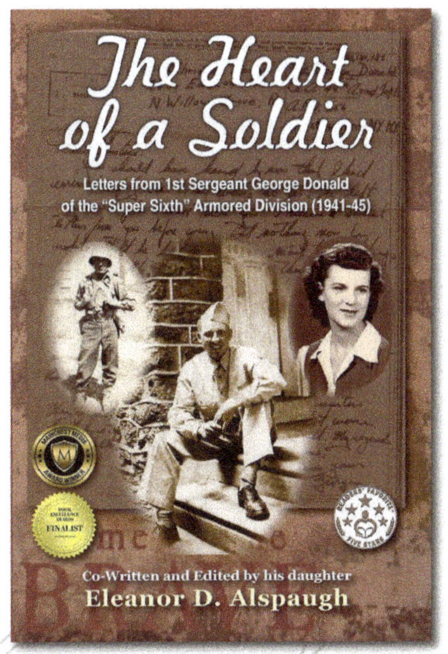

> Eleanor Alspaugh's *The Heart of a Soldier* is a moving blend of personal letters and historical context, capturing Sgt. George Donald's bravery, sacrifices, and enduring love during World War II. Through intimate correspondence and supplemental research, the book offers a heartfelt tribute to the Greatest Generation and their wartime experiences.

Can you share any details about your upcoming projects, such as the sequel to "The Mommy-Go-Round" or your next children's book?

Occasionally, you will hear someone comment that parenting never ends. Well, let me assure you, that is absolutely true! I still find humor sharing life realities that parents experience as their children grow up, marry and eventually become parents themselves. The joy of parenting seriously includes so many unexpected situations that no one warns you about, so stay tuned! Both the sequel and my children's book are making progress. Hopefully, the chaos of parenting and grandparenting will not hold me back too long! Stay tuned!

A Life Transformed By Courage

Award-winning author Hope Brooks reflects on her transformative memoir, A Mother's Survival, sharing heartfelt insights about overcoming trauma, advocating for mental health, and the power of writing to heal.

HOPE BROOKS

SHARES HER JOURNEY OF RESILIENCE AND HEALING THROUGH WRITING

as told to Dan Peters

"Despite the challenges that we face in life, there is always hope."

Deanna Adams needs no introduction—but it is a pleasure to offer one anyway. Writing under her evocative pen name, *Hope Brooks*, this remarkable author has dedicated her craft to the courageous call of chronicling life's most profound struggles and victories. With her deeply moving memoir, *A Mother's Survival: Finding Balance Through the Storms*, she takes her readers on an emotional and inspiring journey. Her words uncover the adversities of a life shaped by trauma, resilience, and unyielding hope, sharing experiences that only the bravest among us could bear to revisit, let alone offer to the world with such honesty and grace.

Hope Brooks has created a voice that speaks not just for herself but for the countless others who have faced life's storms and found a way to rise above. Her memoir reached bestseller status, a testament to her ability to connect with her audience, offering solace and understanding to those who have endured experiences of sexual abuse, the challenges of single parenthood, and the ever-complicated dynamics of raising a blended family. Beyond the book itself, her short story, *Megan's Story*, brings mental health challenges into sharp focus, a subject Hope handles with the same sensitivity and purpose that defines her work.

In this exclusive interview for Reader's House, Hope offers a heartfelt glimpse into the development of her memoir, the personal tribulations that inspired it, and the wisdom she has gained throughout her writing journey. From life's darkest days to the empowering act of finding one's voice, Hope's story is one of transformation, healing, and an unwavering commitment to helping others find their own place of peace. As editor, I'm honoured to bring this conversation to our readers, and I have no doubt that Hope Brooks will leave you inspired by her words, her courage, and her unshakeable sense of purpose.

What inspired you to write "A Mother's Survival: Finding Balance Through the Storms," and how much of it is drawn from your personal experiences?

I had experienced traumatic experiences through most of the days of my life. In childhood, I was a victim of sexual abuse. In my adult years, I became a single parent, alone and searching for a way to feed my children. In my career as a New York City teacher, I faced endless challenges working with special needs children. I often said to myself, "Someday you must write a book, no one would believe what's happening to you." The day after my retirement, I sat down at my computer and began to write, as my life's journey appeared before me.

How do you balance both fiction and nonfiction, and do you have a preference for one over the other?

I have only been drawn to expressing real events and emotions in my writing, and have never been interested in imaginary stories. At another moment in my life, my family faced a crisis when my seven-year-old granddaughter was diagnosed with schizoaffective disorder, an illness with symptoms of both bipolar disorder and schizophrenia. She suffered, hearing voices and not understanding reality or unreal creatures. I felt the world should understand the impact of mental illness on people's lives, and was inspired to write her story, entitled "Megan's Story." This short story has won several awards and can be found on the internet.

> Hope Brooks is an extraordinary storyteller, courageously sharing her life's challenges to inspire readers with hope, strength, and perseverance.

Can you share some of the challenges you faced while writing your book, and how you overcame them?

Having never been an author, I had no knowledge of how to successfully write and turn my words into a memoir. First, I attended some local writing classes for beginners, which I enjoyed. At one of the sessions, a high school English teacher invited me to join his weekly writing group, held at the library. At the meetings, each person read an excerpt of what they had written, while the others critiqued and gave suggestions for ways to improve. This opened a new world for me, as I learned new skills in achieving my writing goals. I attended every week for five years, and finally completed my dream. My advice to new beginners is to find support groups or experienced people who could guide you in your journey, so you are not alone.

How has your background in music and love for rock 'n' roll influenced your writing, particularly in your novels?

Although my novel does not include music, my love of piano and clarinet lessons enabled me to include music in my writing sessions. Each time I sat before my computer to think and type, I sought silent moments, distant from others, as I emotionally relived events from my past. I would often listen to classical composers like Mozart and Beethoven, and their calming pieces became a memorable part of my writing journey.

What advice would you give to aspiring writers who are struggling to find their voice or niche?

Once you have published your book, it is important that you seek organizations comprised of other authors who can share information and advice on how to proceed. When my book was finally in print, I googled nearby author groups who could share my hopes and aspirations. I made a selection and attended my first meeting, finding it to be everything I had hoped for. The activities included scheduled book fairs, presentations by speakers on helpful topics, opportunities to write in monthly publications, online zoom meetings and in person socials. Reaching out to this community, I finally found my niche. This is where I belonged, surrounded by others who were important to me and shared my goals.

How do you approach weaving historical events and pop culture into your story telling without overshadowing the personal narratives?

In Chapter 34, I not only had the opportunity to include a historical event in my pages, but I was also part of it. On the morning of September 11th, 2001, I stood in my Staten Island classroom with my 2nd grade students, and the world as we knew it suddenly changed. From the classroom window we could see the smoke coming from the World Trade Center, and from the loud speaker, the principal announced a school lockdown. Parents came running to rescue their children, and the roads and bridges became blocked by the police. It took me hours in traffic trying to get home from New Jersey. When school reopened a few days later, I faced devastating news. One of my students lost his father, a firefighter at the Twin Towers. Another lost her aunt, who had been unable to escape from the building. A third child lost his soccer coach who had been on the hijacked plane that crashed into the Towers. Sometimes we don't need to weave history into our lives. We just live it, and it remains within us forever.

> Hope Brooks' memoir, *A Mother's Survival: Finding Balance Through the Storms*, is an inspiring account of resilience through childhood trauma, family struggles, and professional challenges. With raw honesty, she shares her journey of perseverance and hope. Though unevenly paced, it's a heartfelt, motivational read offering a compelling testament to human strength.

What words of wisdom or inspiration would you offer to other authors who are navigating the ups and downs of the writing and publishing journey?

One important approach to making sales is to find your target audience. Through the pages of my book, I address the trauma of sexual abuse, being a single parent, remarriage, raising a blended family, and the consequences of bitter divorce on your children and stepchildren. When I attend book fairs and set up my table, those are the words I use on my poster to attract my buyers. It gives me meaning and satisfaction to verbally interact with others who have had similar experiences. I now have a plan for my book's success. I want to have it made into a movie, a successful movie that addresses so many issues in today's society. I have submitted it to literary agents and producers, but as of now I've been rejected. I ask myself, "Should I give up?" The answer is NO.

From Metropolitan Police Veteran To Best-Selling Novels

Jonathan Cox, acclaimed for his Nostrils series, reflects on blending realism with fiction, crafting flawed anti-heroes, and drawing upon his covert operations and personal experiences for gripping, authentic police procedurals.

JONATHAN COX

CHALLENGES CONVENTION WITH BOLD, CINEMATIC STORYTELLING

"My knowledge of the dark arts enabled me to write with accuracy and authenticity without compromising proactive policing operations."

as told to Dan Peters

Jonathan Cox, a distinguished and celebrated author, brings to life his unparalleled literary journey anchored in his extensive and authentic policing career. With his debut work, *The Blue Trilogy*, conceived immediately after his retirement from the Metropolitan Police in 2013, Cox quickly established himself as a monumental force in modern British crime fiction. Originally imagined as a three-book series, the resounding success of these novels inspired five additional instalments, expanding the series into a remarkable eight-book saga that has captivated readers across generations and professions alike.

At the heart of his literary prowess lies *From Green to Blue*, the first work in the series, which has claimed UK No.1 Best Seller status across an impressive array of Amazon categories, including General Fiction, Humour, and Police Procedurals. Cox's deeply rooted experiences as an investigator of police and public sector corruption infuse his novels with a realism and authenticity that simply cannot be replicated. Perhaps this is why the Nostrils series, named after its flawed yet endearing protagonist PC Chris Pritchard, has resonated so profoundly within the law enforcement community, becoming a cult classic among serving and retired police officers.

Cox's commitment to crafting grounded, multifaceted characters, like the anti-hero Pritchard, reflects his belief that humanity is an intricate weave of light and shade—a concept he masterfully explores across his series. Navigating themes of integrity, moral ambiguity, and camaraderie under high-pressure circumstances, Cox seamlessly blends gripping narratives with a nuanced exploration of the human condition.

Beyond the realism of his stories, Jonathan Cox's extensive service in divisions ranging from murder squads and financial intelligence units to covert counter-terrorism operations offers an unmatched depth to his storytelling. His authentic portrayal of both the gritty and the often unseen complexities of police work sets his fiction apart in an increasingly crowded genre. His ability to channel his decades of high-stakes experience into riveting page-turners ensures that every book feels like a vivid account of life on the frontline.

Whether he is detailing the intricate dance of corruption investigations or exploring the emotional trials faced by those in the force, Cox balances his role as an unwavering custodian of truth with the demands of mesmerizing fiction. His success is a testament not just to his talent but to his passion for preserving and presenting the raw realities of policing. For anyone seeking a truly authentic voice in crime fiction, Jonathan Cox's works are simply unmissable.

In this issue of *Reader's House*, we are privileged to delve into the mind of the UK's pre-eminent writer of police procedurals. Join us in celebrating Jonathan Cox—a storyteller of unrivalled authenticity and impact—and prepare to experience a captivating blend of gritty realism and poignant humanity.

What inspired you to write about police corruption in the 1980s Metropolitan Police, and how much of your personal experience influenced the storylines?

I spent over twenty years of my life investigating corruption in a variety of organisations, in the UK and abroad, so the topic is both my Mastermind specialist subject and my passion. For me, the particularly interesting aspect about 1980's police corruption is the malpractice known as 'noble cause corruption', where the person undertaking the activity makes no personal gain, and they genuinely believe what they are doing is for the greater good of society. There is, however, an inseparable but fascinating link between noble cause of acquisitional corruption which From Green to Blue examines in some detail.

> A master storyteller, Cox blends authenticity with riveting narratives, offering unparalleled insights into the world of policing through his critically acclaimed novels.

Your character Chris Pritchard is described as an anti-hero - what made you choose this complex characterisation rather than a more traditional heroic protagonist?

No one is perfect. We are all a mix of good and bad, light and dark. So, it was essential my protagonist reflected reality, someone many of us on some level can relate to. Besides, anti-heroes are far more complex, and I have always found them more captivating than their goody-goody counterparts. During the Nostrils Series (spoiler alert), PC Pritchard does some truly awful things, but there is always an underlying reason. I want to make the reader think, yes, I would have done that, too. Even when the activity itself is quite appalling. Very aptly a reviewer once wrote, 'PC Pritchard is a character more flawed by events than his own nature', which epitomises Nostrils precisely.

How did your experience in witness protection and covert operations shape the authenticity of your narratives?

My knowledge of the dark arts enabled me to write with accuracy and authenticity. I knew what was capable of being done and, more importantly, in what circumstances such activities would be authorised. In my time, I specialised in directed and intrusive surveillance, so these tactics appear sporadically throughout the series. I was, however, always conscious not to overstep the mark by exposing activities and capabilities that are not widely known. I was keen not to compromise any current or future proactive policing operations.

The relationship between PC Pritchard and WPC Dawn Matthews is quite central to the first book - was this based on any real-life mentorship you experienced?

Absolutely it was! My real mentor when I had just started on the force, was a WPC called Karen who was an outstanding police officer. I was an arrogant, ignorant, nineteen-year-old who'd inherited his father's misogynistic and racist views. Quite understandably, therefore, she had little time for me. Unlike the main characters in From Green to Blue, however, our real relationship didn't really improve. Thirty years later and after I'd published, I found Karen on social media, and we formed a friendship that has endured ever since. I know she would like me to point out that, unlike the fictitious Dawn, she never had a relationship with a married man!

Given your extensive career investigating corruption, how challenging was it to balance the need for realism with the requirements of engaging fiction?

I made a promise to myself that I would write credibly and would always reflect accurate policing practice. All my plots therefore have a firm foothold in truth. I never found an issue balancing realism with engaging fiction for the simple reason that being a police officer was such an incredibly interesting job I didn't have to make anything up. Indeed, ninety percent of From Green to Blue happened, maybe not to me, but certainly to others with whom I worked. Consequently, my books possess that vital ingredient of realism, so often missing from similar tales penned by those who, although far more accomplished writers, have never actually done the job.

Your books have become particularly popular among serving and retired officers - what feedback from this audience has meant the most to you?

I am extremely lucky to regularly receive positive feedback from my readers, via published reviews, and also through private messaging on social media. When I receive a complimentary communication from a former colleague the memories of our times together come flooding back. Friendships forged in the heat of battle are always the strongest, and while we weren't at war, sometimes when you are policing a busy city, it can feel that way. With that said, when a reader without any policing background writes that they have been thrilled to have had a police career vicariously through PC Pritchard, I get equally emotional.

> Jonathan Cox's From Green to Blue delivers an authentic, humour-filled portrayal of policing in London's East End. With vivid characters, sharp dialogue, and poignant themes, the book balances raw realism with heartfelt moments. Though pacing occasionally falters, it's an honest, engaging read that reflects the camaraderie and challenges of police life.

What advice would you give to other retired police officers who are considering writing about their experiences in law enforcement?

Go for it! What have you got to lose? At the very least, you will have captured your memories for friends and family, and future generations, to read. At best, you might have penned a best-seller. Writing fiction is possibly more fun, because there is more freedom to 'play' with your storylines and sub-plots. It is also safer, as you shouldn't end up in court. I would be happy to talk to anyone thinking about doing so, just send me an email or message. Personally, it is a thrilling experience to sit in front of a blank page and type the following nine characters 'Chapter 1'. An experience only matched in excitement when one finds oneself, several months later, frantically writing the climax to the story into the early hours of the morning.

Folklore, Fantasy, And Family

Kate Church discusses her passion for folklore, the creation of morally complex fantasy worlds, and the heartfelt inspiration behind *Splat the Dinosaur*, a story of kindness and self-acceptance.

"I enjoyed bending traditional tropes or adding my own twists to them. It is why I love fiction—there are no rules."

KATE CHURCH

INSPIRES READERS WITH FANTASY WORLDS, FOLKLORE, AND A DINOSAUR NAMED SPLAT

as told to Ben Alan

Few authors manage to weave the threads of imagination, history, and humanity as seamlessly as Kate Church. A masterful storyteller with a penchant for the fantastical, Kate has carved a unique niche in the literary world, blending her love of folklore, medieval history, and boundless creativity into works that both challenge and enchant. From the sweeping landscapes of *The Chronicles of Caladh* to the heartfelt charm of *Splat the Dinosaur,* her stories resonate with readers of all ages, offering not just escapism but profound reflections on the human experience.

Her debut novel, A Breath Before Drowning, marked the arrival of a bold new voice in fantasy fiction, while *Seeking the Wolf*and its sequel, *Lifting the Veil*, have cemented her reputation as a visionary in the genre. With shapeshifters, hidden alliances, and morally complex characters, Kate's work pushes the boundaries of traditional fantasy, inviting readers to explore worlds where power shifts unexpectedly and nothing is as it seems.

But Kate's talents are not confined to the realm of dark fantasy. Her children's book, *Splat the Dinosaur*, is a testament to her versatility and her deeply personal connection to storytelling. Co-created with her son, Zac, *Splat* is more than a tale of self-acceptance and kindness—it's a beacon of hope and understanding for children and families navigating the challenges of autism. Through school visits and storytelling sessions, Kate and Zac have brought Splat's message to life, fostering awareness and compassion in communities far and wide.

In this issue of *Reader's House*, we delve into the mind of this

> Kate Church's Seeking the Wolf is a masterful blend of dark fantasy and intricate world-building. With morally complex characters and a gripping plot, this tale of power, pride, and shapeshifters captivates from start to finish. Church's vivid imagination and storytelling prowess make this a must-read for fantasy enthusiasts.

extraordinary author. From the Celtic folklore that inspires her fantasy worlds to the heartfelt journey behind *Splat the Dinosaur*, Kate Church shares the stories behind her stories. Prepare to be inspired by her passion, her creativity, and her unwavering belief in the power of storytelling to connect, heal, and transform.

Kate Church is not just an author; she is a force of nature, a voice for the unheard, and a creator of worlds that linger long after the final page is turned. It is our privilege to bring you this exclusive interview with a writer whose work reminds us why we read—and why we dream.

What specific folklore or medieval historical events have inspired your writing, and how do you incorporate these elements into the worlds you create?

While I study folklore from around the world, I tend to be drawn towards that of Northern Europe, particularly Celtic folklore,

> Kate Church is a literary marvel, blending folklore, history, and heartfelt storytelling to create unforgettable worlds and characters.

where I feel my connection is strongest. That accompanied by my fascination and research into the Middle Ages of the same region allows me to embrace the culture along with architectural and other historical findings to provide a guideline for what will be.

As a healthcare worker, how does your professional experience influence your storytelling in fantasy fiction, particularly in terms of character development and themes?

I do not believe it has influenced my work in the least. I have been an artist all my life and writing was just another form my art has taken. While my characters, creatures and worlds are created of my own imagination and/or experience, the fact that I have worked in healthcare has held no merit in the development of my work.

What inspired you to create the world of Caladh and the concept of shapeshifters in Seeking the Wolf?

Being an avid fantasy reader since I was young, part of what had drawn me to writing was the ability to fill in gaps or tell stories that I had yet to encounter in literature. While The Chronicles of Caladh has several of the traditional tropes found amongst other works of fantasy, I enjoyed bending those tropes or adding my own twists to them. It is why I love fiction. There are no rules and each storyteller has the ability to create a world all their own.

How do the themes of power and pride in Seeking the Wolf reflect the current challenges we face in our own society?

We have all bore witness to an abuse of power or the pride grown too strong for one's own good. I think in a way Seeking the Wolf reflects a lifetime of those occurrences however vast or insignificant they may have seemed at the time. Since my writing draws from my own experiences it would be only natural for some of those subconscious thoughts or feelings to seep their way into some of the characters.

What challenges did you face while developing the plot and character dynamics in Lifting the Veil, particularly with themes of hidden intentions and alliances?

The biggest challenge I faced in developing the plotline and characters in a series was cohesiveness and consistency. I took extensive notes on the verbiage used by the characters, created bios for each as several of the characters have some sort of connection that may or may not be apparent depending on where in the series you are at and even created a map to help better navigate the world as I was telling the story.

In Lifting the Veil, how do you explore the idea of power shifting through unlikely individuals, and what message do you hope readers take away from this?

I choose to write Dark Fantasy as characters often tend to be morally ambiguous allowing the reader to determine for themselves how they choose to see those characters. I explored this idea a great deal for nearly two years before Lifting the Veil came into existence. That accompanied with the idea that we rarely know those around us created the mold that builds a growing curiosity when a new character is introduced, or something previously thought to be unremarkable gains a foothold.

What inspired you to create a story about a dinosaur who struggles with being different, and how did you develop Splat's character to convey themes of self-acceptance and kindness?

My son was diagnosed with autism several years ago and as we ventured to therapy every week, we used to tell each other stories as we drove. Sometimes we would even create a story together and that was how Splat was born. He would add a piece of the story and then I would add another and so on until the story was complete. Initially, I believed that Splat was my son's way of expressing how he felt the world treated him and being autistic myself, I could relate to this. In truth, my son is Splat and through his eyes he wants the world to be more kind even if we do not always understand, appear or act like one another. Each person is given the opportunity to be kind and accept those as they are, but that opportunity is often discarded when it should not be. I never intended to publish the story, but the more I spoke of the story the more interest grew. Splat has become a comfort to so many and in the spirit of kindness my son and I use this project to spread kindness and let others like ourselves know that they are not alone.

Can you share any insights into the creative process behind the book, particularly how you approached illustrating Splat's journey and the challenges he faces?

Seeing how the book was designed for children and partially created by a child, bright colors were the logical choice to make the story appealing for all ages. In addition, since autism is not always visually apparent, my son and I decided to make Splat's differences physical to better convey the meaning behind the story rather than relying on subtext. After sifting through several illustrators, I stumbled upon Caleb Peregrine, an autistic artist from the UK. With his background in paleontology and watercolors, Splat no longer was just in our imagination, but a beautiful character created by the minds of three autistic individuals.

The Journey Behind Six Brilliant Novels

Len Joy reflects on his evolution from businessman to award-winning author, blending athletics, resilience, and life experiences into six novels that explore relationships, legacies, and the beauty of small-town America.

LEN JOY

AWARD-WINNING AUTHOR SHARES INSIGHTS ON WRITING, LIFE, AND TRIUMPH

as told to Dan Peters

"Be honest, but considerate. Be kind."

Len Joy's name has become synonymous with powerful storytelling, unforgettable characters, and the nuanced depiction of life in small town America. With a career that has blossomed later in life, Len has proven that it's never too late to chase your dreams. A former athlete, business owner, and now an acclaimed author, he brings a wealth of experience to his writing, crafting stories that resonate with universality while steeped in authenticity.

With six remarkable novels under his belt, Len has created a body of work that explores the depth and complexity of human relationships, personal resilience, and the passage of time. His debut, *American Past Time*, introduced readers to the Stonemason family, a multi generational saga full of triumph and tragedy. *Everyone Dies Famous* brought a haunting yet hopeful continuation of this story, while his latest, *American Jukebox,* delves further into the legacy of the Stonemason family, showcasing Len's extraordinary ability to capture small town life and its ripple effects across generations.

Beyond the Stonemason trilogy, Len's stand alone works have also received high praise. From the compulsively readable *Freedom's Just Another Word...* to the gripping and heartfelt *Dry Heat*, not to mention the masterful wryness of *Better Days,* Len blends humour, heartbreak, and humanity with ease. Each novel is a testament to his sharp insight into the human condition and his gift for crafting narratives that linger long after the final page.

In this exclusive interview, we explore the journey of a writer who has transformed himself over the decades, turning rejection into fuel for success. Len's experiences, both on the page and in life, are as compelling as the worlds he creates in his books. Whether you are a longtime fan or a newcomer to his work, this conversation promises to illuminate the mind behind the novels and inspire anyone with the spark of an untold story.

Tell us about your writer's journey.

When I went off to college (many years ago) I was an English major and planned to become a world famous bestselling novelist. But after my American Lit professor excoriated my term paper on Thoreau, my writerly ambitions were crushed, and I switched my major to Economics and went to business school.

I eventually bought an engine rebuilding company in Phoenix and for twenty years I commuted between Chicago and Phoenix. After we wound the business down in 2003, on a whim, I took a creative writing course. I got just enough encouragement that I took more courses. In 2007 I started working on a novel. It took me seven years, but in 2014, American Past Time was published.

It is the story of minor league pitcher Dancer Stonemason. With his wife and son cheering him on, he pitches the greatest game of his life. And then loses everything. Told against the backdrop of America's postwar challenges from Little Rock to the Bay of Pigs to Viet Nam, American Past Time is the story of what happens to a man and his family after the cheering stops.

Len Joy masterfully crafts compelling, heartfelt stories, capturing the essence of human connection and the struggles that shape our lives.

The Stonemason family shows up again in your 3rd novel, Everyone Dies Famous.

In my earlier drafts, American Past Time was a multi generational family epic, but that was too ambitious for a debut novel. I cut the scope so it would end in 1976. Dancer Stonemason is the main character in Everyone Dies Famous, but he is now a griefstricken seventy year old. The story takes place on a single day in July 2003. As a tornado threatens their small Missouri town, Dancer teams up with an Iraq war veteran to deliver a jukebox to a wealthy developer who is having an affair with the soldier's wife. Bad things happen.

A jukebox. Interesting. Your latest novel is American Jukebox. Another Stonemason story?

Yes. American Jukebox is Clayton Stonemason story. It covers some of the same ground as American Past Time, but from Clayton's perspective. Clayton idolized his father, a hometown hero in their small Missouri town. But when his father's life unravels, Clayton loses his way, too. He tries to escape his father's legacy but discovers he can't run from his destiny. It is a story of smalltown America in the last decades of the twentieth century, that explores the many ways our relationships, hopes, and dreams can alter the course of our lives.

So you have a trilogy?

Yes, just like J. K. Rowling. But all the Stonemason stories are standalone novels.

You're a triathlete and a member of TEAM USA. How has that influenced your writing?

They're complementary activities. Both require discipline and training. I have a coach to help me become a better athlete, and I've had countless instructors, writers, and editors who have helped me to become a better writer. All my novels feature athletes. A general theme I explore is the life lived after the cheering stops.

Your Phoenix-based novel, Dry Heat is a love story. What was the inspiration for that tale?

The protagonist of Dry Heat is Joey Blade, a promising high school athlete who is falsely accused of shooting a cop. He enlists the aid of a notorious gang leader to find the real shooter, unleashing a chain of events that alters the course of his life and that of the girl he loves. I worked in Phoenix for twenty years and the story, while fictional, is inspired by a real event that happened to one of my employees.

Your novel Better Days has been described as an "attention-grabbing crime story." How do you craft compelling plots that keep readers engaged from start to finish?

Better Days is the story of Darwin Burr, a man who has coasted for years on the fading glory of his high school basketball success. The novel has marital discord, shady business dealings, corporate intrigue, gang warfare, and most important, girls high school basketball. It was a rewarding challenge to keep all those plates spinning and bring the story to a satisfactory conclusion. Well, at least I was satisfied. Some readers hated the ending, but I prefer hate to indifference.

In "Freedom's Just Another Word...", you explore complex family dynamics. What inspired you to delve into these intricate relationships?

Jake Doyle, the main character in Freedom's Just Another Word... used to be famous. Twenty years ago, his Chicago political column was syndicated in two hundred papers, but he had an affair – and a son – with his intern and lost it all. Now he writes a local column and drives for Uber to pay his bills. The book has a lot of hotbutton issues: abortion, biracial families, gang wars, wokeness. It's not a polemic – it's the story of a 20th century man trying to survive in a 21st century world. I was inspired to write about a newspaperman, because I love newspapers, and I'm sad to see them fade away.

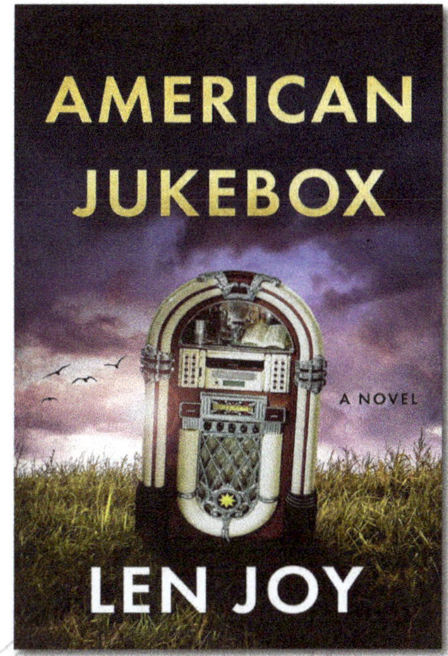

A beautifully written, character-driven story that masterfully explores family, identity, and resilience with heartfelt emotion and relatable depth.

What advice do you have for aspiring writers?

My writing career was squelched early on by harsh criticism. Looking back, I now understand that it wasn't that harsh. I was a sensitive young man who wasn't ready to be a writer. After thirty years in the business world, I was more resilient and more experienced. Delaying my writing career helped me.

I have learned from that experience to not take criticism to heart. Use what is useful and ignore the rest. And when offering critiques of other writer's work, be honest, but considerate. Be kind.

Rootlessness, Noir, and the Art of Reinventing Worlds

Leonce Gaiter discusses how his dynamic upbringing, historical imagination, and love of jazz inspire his bold, character-driven narratives that seamlessly explore race, identity, and societal dynamics across thrilling worlds.

"Jazz is so exciting because it's dangerous—it's emotionally kaleidoscopic, just like my writing."

LEONCE GAITER

CHALLENGES CONVENTION WITH BOLD, CINEMATIC STORYTELLING

as told to Z. Roberts

Leonce Gaiter stands as a consummate storyteller, deftly weaving together complex characters, morally intricate narratives, and vibrant, deeply evocative settings. Boasting a career that spans multiple creative spheres—from literature to film, music, and even tech—Gaiter brings an unparalleled richness to his work. His prose is bold and unapologetic, unearthing the raw, unresolved tensions of race, power, and identity through the lens of history, noir, and psychological depth. Titles such as *I Dreamt I Was in Heaven – The Rampage of the Rufus Buck Gang*, *Bourbon Street,* and *In the Company of Educated Men* demonstrate his gift for reimagining historical moments and unflinching human truths, presented with cinematic flair and intellectual vigour.

With the forthcoming release of *A Memory of Fictions,* a lyrical blend of memoir and fiction, Gaiter has once again proven why he is celebrated as a risk-taker in contemporary literature. His work challenges genre conventions, embraces emotional and cultural nuance, and captivates readers with stories that simultaneously transport and provoke. Whether tracing the ragged jazz-like rhythms of a young man's coming of age or peeling back the layers of New Orleans's atmospheric allure, Gaiter effortlessly immerses his audience in worlds as dangerous as they are beautiful. In this issue of *Reader's House*, we sit down with the award-winning author to delve into his creative process, his literary influences, and his unflinching exploration of the human condition. It is a conversation not to be missed.

How has your upbringing as an "army brat" influenced your writing style and the themes you explore in your books?

Rootlessness is the word the comes to mind. For me, moving often from place to place instilled a sense of instability, and moving from place to place as a black family in the 60s meant anxiety. You never knew what kind of reception you'd receive at a new school as an individual, or, in many cases, as a black one. My characters are often trying to make environments safe for themselves, trying to construct a home, using the only tools they've been taught—tools that include violence.

There's also the question of authority: I'm generally against it, and I'm only half kidding. Son of a military man with a very military mindset, my own bent runs toward exploration and constant questioning. I always chafed at "that's the way it is," responses. My characters tend to do the same. My New Orleans southern roots instilled a sense of the gothic and overripe, so I write larger than life characters often in life and death situations, and most of them are trying to rewrite the worlds they live in, upend the established order, often to create world they're comfortable calling home.

Your novel A Memory of Fictions (or) Just Tiddy-Boom has been described as both lyrical and bold—how did you approach blending memoir and fiction in this work?

Leonce Gaiter is a literary force, crafting unforgettable characters and immersive settings with unparalleled vision, emotional resonance, and intellectual daring.

Several times I've recalled an event to my sibling who has then shared a radically different reading of the same event. We filter our memories through our emotions, prejudices, and other factors we can't even identify. I knew anything I wrote that touched on events in my own life would be inaccurate, so I leaned into that and used some events in my life as a foundation for an intimate, yet expansive tale that traces the personal, intellectual, and sexual coming of age of young man from the civil rights '60s through the Reagan '80s.

I am a jazz fanatic and this book in particular references that obsession. Jazz is so exciting because it's dangerous. It's held together by sheer talent and with a lapse the whole thing could fall apart. It's unpredictable, and it is emotionally kaleidoscopic. There is no one "tone" in jazz, or in much of African American music. It can be sad one second, ironic the next, and mocking right after that. I think this book is called "bold" because it, too, is emotionally and structurally kaleidoscopic.

Bourbon Street is deeply rooted in the atmosphere of New Orleans—how did you capture the city's essence, and what role does setting play in your storytelling?

The time I spent in New Orleans is particularly vivid for me, and not necessarily for good reasons. I took that sense of place from my young memories and built the story around it. "Bourbon Street" is my love letter to film noir, and novelists like Jim Thompson and Patricia Highsmith. Setting in my books is always an outgrowth of character. You might say my characters project the world around them. The characters and the world they inhabit reflect and feed off each other.

Your work often delves into themes of race, identity, and societal expectations—how do you balance historical accuracy with creative storytelling in your historical novels?

When I read historical fiction, I am rarely impressed with writers' showing off their research. I'm more drawn to a distinct sense of cultural and emotional place within that timeframe. What is this author's vision of the old west, or Edwardian England? As with memory, historical information will always be filtered through our personal lenses. In historical fiction, I write to immerse you in my take on that period as reflected through characters. I'm less interested in the objective temporal details.

And I don't think I deal with "identity" per se. I think my characters exist within their identities. There's a difference. When I write black characters, I don't write about them being black, which is one definition of writing from a white frame. I write characters who are black. And those black characters assume power. They take for granted they have the power to alter the world around them, and they act to do so with the same sense of righteousness that any white person would.

You've worked in film, music, and tech—how have these experiences shaped your approach to writing and storytelling?

I sincerely hope working adjacent to tech has not influenced me in any way whatsoever. With respect to film, I've been told my work is very cinematic, but strangely unfilmable. I think the world-building of film—particularly classical Hollywood films—really influenced me, but I project that influence through the writing style. I guess that's the unfilmable part.

What do you hope readers take away from your exploration of complex characters and morally ambiguous narratives?

First, I hope readers are entertained. I hope they see worlds they're not accustomed to, peopled with fascinating characters who live in accord with this new world. I hope they take from my work the memory of unique characters sprayed on a larger-than-life canvas.

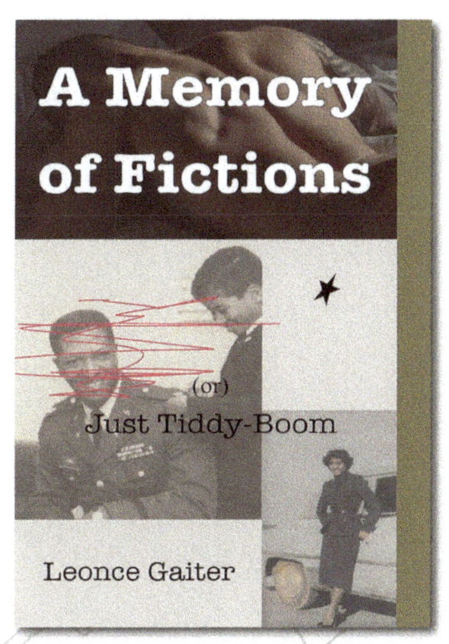

Leonce Gaiter's *A Memory of Fictions* is a powerful, postmodern exploration of race, sexuality, and identity. Through experimental, evocative prose, it portrays Jessie Vincent Grandier's struggles with societal and familial expectations. Bold and intimate, this unforgettable novel blends honesty, tenderness, and redemption in a masterful, genre-defying narrative.

A Journey Through World War II, Science Fiction, and Creative Writing

Dr Mike Hollows discusses his historical and speculative fiction, the challenges of genre-switching, and his passion for teaching creative writing while reflecting on history's lessons and his personal journey.

M.J. HOLLOWS

EXPLORES HISTORY, HUMANITY, AND THE ART OF STORYTELLING ACROSS GENRES

as told to Dan Peters

"The main reason I chose to explore World War II was because we still have a lot to learn from the past.'

Dr Mike Hollows is a name that has become synonymous with versatility, depth, and an unwavering passion for the written word. A highly accomplished author and doctor of creative writing, Mike, writes as M. J. Hollows has made an indelible mark across multiple literary landscapes, crafting historical fiction, science fiction, and fantasy with equal mastery. His body of work, published through notable platforms such as Harper Collins' HQStories and Games Workshop's Black Library, is an extraordinary testament to his ability to traverse genres while retaining his signature narrative power.

From the poignant historical narratives of *Goodbye for Now* and *The German Nurse* to his gripping World War II explorations in *The Violinist's Secret* and *The German Messenger,* Mike transports readers into vividly realised chapters of history, unearthing both the human spirit and its frailty. Meanwhile, his ventures into speculative realms, such as *The Warp's Curse* and *Ashes of Grimnir*, are evidence of his remarkable talent for conjuring imaginative worlds that are as immersive as they are thought-provoking.

A scholar with an unquenchable thirst for understanding storytelling's complexities, Mike's academic achievements underpin his creative expertise. His PhD exploring the Golden Age of Science Fiction and his ongoing studies in Creative Writing Pedagogy continue to influence his work, providing intriguing layers for all who delve into his narratives. It is this commitment to research and his insightful examination of socio-political themes—be it the echoes of wartime resilience, neurodivergent experiences, or the human condition—that sets him apart from his contemporaries.

In this exclusive interview, Dr Hollows offers a glimpse into the processes that shape his celebrated works, from the meticulous historical research behind his novels to his seamless genre-switching prowess. Whether discussing his inspirations, his approach to character creation, or his advice for writers looking to step into multifaceted literary worlds, Mike's thoughtful reflections are a gift to readers and aspiring authors alike. It is with immense pride and admiration that we shine a spotlight on this award-winning storyteller, whose pen continues to illuminate and inspire.

What inspired you to explore World War II themes in *"The Violinist's Secret"* and *"The German Messenger"*?

The main reason I chose to explore World War II was because we still have a lot to learn from the past. Sadly, we have come only so far from these lessons, and with the apparent rise of populism and xenophobia in our world it's important to revisit the past and explore what has happened before.

The Violinist's Secret is a bit of a departure from my World War II novels set in British territories, but I wanted to explore a woman's role in Nazi Germany. When the Nazis came to power many German institutions were at the forefront of various areas of research, and there were a number of women included in this research. The Nazis, however, wanted women to be wives and mothers, and so I asked myself, 'how did this play out?' I was almost certain that not every woman would be happy with these twin roles and sought to tell that story.

> MJ Hollows is a literary powerhouse whose captivating storytelling, intellectual depth, and genre-spanning talent continue to mesmerise readers worldwide.

The German Messenger came about a different way. Liverpool was the second most bombed city in England during World War II, but this is never talked about. It was also a study of human nature that resonated with the Covid pandemic. During the Blitz, not everyone followed the rules, and I wanted to explore this. It was amazing during my research how similar it felt. Everyone was scared and that played out in odd ways.

How do you balance historical accuracy with the creative demands of storytelling in your novels?

I'm fortunate in my historical novels that, firstly, they are set in the relatively recent past, so there is a lot of research on which to draw and, secondly, that I can structure them around a real timeline. This gives a sense of historical accuracy, that the narrative events happen against a backdrop of real events. I also make sure I read as many accounts from the time as possible and see what sorts of things may happen in my own story. But I have had some truth is stranger than fiction moments. The key, I think, is to ask yourself what theme you are trying to explore in this section and then make sure that the scene is something that could plausibly have happened at the time.

Can you share your process for developing characters like Charlotte Weber and ensuring they resonate with readers?

I spend a lot of time researching character names and this is important because they not only have to sound right, but names also form a sort of archetype. When I am writing point of view characters I almost close my eyes and imagine what it would have been like to live in their world. That way I can describe everything as if they were living it. Making sure characters resonate with readers isn't about making them likeable, but it's about giving readers something to empathise with. If the character is feeling the world around them then the reader will too.

What challenges do you face when switching between genres like historical fiction, science fiction, and fantasy?

I think there is a lot of similarity. The main challenge of writing any genre fiction is making sure that it feels it is of a time. So, in historical fiction, something as simple as a hat stand, which we don't tend to see any more, gives the reader a sense of time. In fantasy it could be an arming rack, in science fiction a space suit. The challenge is in making them feel like real worlds. That's the colour. Then the stories told within these worlds is what gives the nuance and individuality. And each story is different.

What is your most valuable piece of advice for other authors aspiring to write across multiple genres successfully?

I would say ask yourself why you are writing in this genre. Each of them has a role to play in narrative and exploration. They're not just window dressing. So, for historical fiction it might be a case of exploring why something may have happened in our past or, as I've mentioned, what we've failed to learn. For science fiction it could be a way of exploring our own world but using a different lens that allows us objective distance from the issue at hand. And fantasy, although I treat fantasy and science fiction as two styles of the same genre, it could be a way of exploring how people might be different if they lived in a different world. Don't just write it because you like reading it, but understand what is at the core of that genre. Then you will be able to write across genres as you know which will best fit the story you are trying to tell.

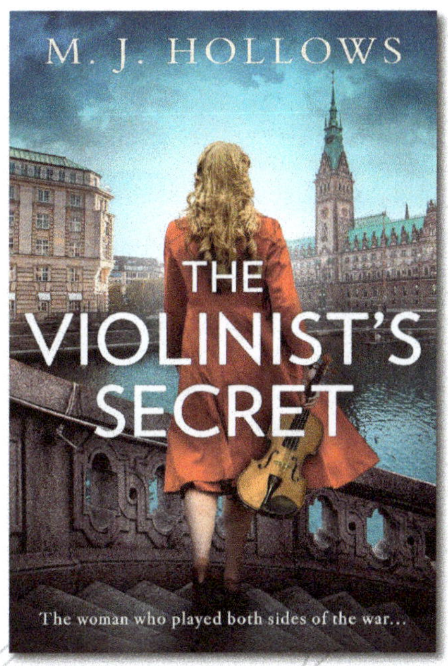

> A gripping World War II spy novel, *The Violinist's Secret* masterfully blends suspense, historical detail, and moral complexity. Charlotte's compelling journey, atmospheric writing, and engaging twists shine, despite occasional pacing issues. M.J. Hollows delivers an authentic, thought-provoking tale perfect for fans of historical fiction and espionage. A solid 4-star read!

A Journey Of Passion And Persistence

Award-winning author Marcy Bialeschki discusses her creative process, the growth of her iconic characters, the triumphs of her writing career, and invaluable advice for aspiring writers in this engaging interview.

MARCY BIALESCHKI

DISCUSSES HER JOURNEY, INSPIRATIONS, AND THE SECRETS BEHIND THE VENGEANCE SERIES

as told to Dan Peters

> "I have said from the beginning, 'You'll want a love like Aria and Mac.' And I still believe that 100%!"

Marcy Bialeschki is an exceptional talent in the literary world, and it is our privilege here at *Reader's House* to feature her in this issue. With an impressive ability to blend romance and suspense into deeply compelling narratives, Marcy has captivated readers with her 4-book romance-suspense masterpiece, *The Vengeance Series*. Her first instalment, *Deception & Consequences*, not only claimed the number one spot in its genre on Ingram merely eleven days after its release but also earned well-deserved acclaim by securing the Literary Titan Award, the Publisher's Choice Award, and the International Impact Book Award for Books in a Series. Since then, Marcy has continued to carve her own path, painting vibrant characters and gripping storylines that have left her readers eagerly yearning for more.

Not one to rest on her laurels, Marcy's influence extends far beyond her novels. She has stepped into the arena of public speaking, sharing her wisdom and experiences at events like the prestigious Women's Thrive Summit, and she has also delved into entrepreneurial ventures through her online platform, Tastefully Sexy by MarcyB. With a career spanning 36 years in education, where her love for teaching writing and literature became an indelible part of her identity, Marcy's sheer passion for storytelling permeates all her creative endeavours. Her upcoming standalone novel, *Where No One Will Look,* promises yet another whirlwind of suspense and emotion, and there is much more on the horizon with another title slated before the close of 2025.

In this interview, Marcy pulls back the curtain on her creative process, her journey as an author, and the extraordinary characters she has brought to life. From the serendipitous beginnings of *The Vengeance Series* to the challenges and triumphs of her publishing journey, she offers an inspiring glimpse into her world. It's a conversation teeming with passion, authenticity, and invaluable wisdom for both her readers and aspiring authors. Marcy is, without a doubt, a force of nature in modern storytelling, and we are delighted to share her story with you.

What inspired you to start writing the Vengeance Series?

Honestly, I'm not sure that I decided to write a novel. I mean I always wanted to write one, but I didn't actively say one day, "Hey, it's time to write that book!" But I remember the idea for the plot coming into my head and dismissing it at first. When more and more ideas downloaded at rapid speed, I couldn't ignore them anymore. I had to start getting it all on paper.

Can you share the creative process behind developing the characters of Mac and Aria?

I poured my heart and soul into creating Mac and Aria and developing their relationship. I wanted Aria to make a phenomenal transformation from beginning to end. She begins as a completely ordinary woman who gets thrown into a life-changing, dangerous situation and has to adjust; and not only adjust but also stay one step ahead of the bad guys. With every perilous situation, Aria must be stronger to survive, and she rises to the occasion. In the end, she's a bad ass, and never looks back.

> Marcy Bialeschki is a masterful storyteller whose compelling narratives and inspiring journey continue to resonate deeply with readers worldwide.

In the beginning, Mac is Aria's guardian angel and protector. By the end, they are equal partners. Mac is every woman's dream! Instead of feeling insecure and threatened by her new independence, Mac just loves her more. For Mac, Aria's growth is the ultimate compliment. Where she needs Mac's guidance and protection initially, she wants him in the end, and there's a big difference. I have said from the beginning, "You'll want a love like Aria and Mac." And I still believe that 100%!

How did the decision to change the ending of Deception & Consequences impact the direction of the series?

Deception & Consequences was supposed to be a stand-alone novel, but I wasn't ready to let go of my characters. Mac and Aria had an entire life together that I wanted to create. I was literally typing the last paragraphs of the book, and I had a thought. When I finished the new ending and reread it, I got chills. That's when I knew I made the right decision.

The second and third books, Seduction and Revenge and Nightmares & Premonitions, continue telling the story. I wrote the last book, Secrets & Infidelity, to keep all the series details straight in my mind. I needed to go back in time before Aria and explain how the whole messy family feud began, so the series made sense in my mind. I knew that if I couldn't connect all the dots, my readers couldn't either. So, the interquel was a self-serving checklist. Besides, CiCi Halprin had become such a strong influence in the series, even I wanted more of her. And that's what Secrets & Infidelity offers.

What challenges did you face when transitioning from self-publishing to collaborating with Words Matter Publishing?

I know very successful authors who self-publish, but it wasn't my forte. For me, there were no challenges in the transition, only relief. I'm not a content formatter, a cover designer, or an editor. I don't know the first thing about the business of selling books. I'm a writer, and I want to focus my attention on doing what I love and what I do best. When Words Matter Publishing picked up my series, my books got the professional attention and presentation they deserve. I am blessed.

How did you develop the suspenseful and romantic elements of your writing to keep readers engaged?

I spent 36 years teaching writing, and I still struggle explaining the process of pacing and creating suspense. So, instead, I'll explain why my books are just one big disaster after another. I hate boring lulls in books. Keep me engaged. Keep me thinking. When I find myself writing aimlessly, creating that boring lull I hate so much, I stop writing. I want drama, danger, tension, and fear through the entire book. I'll admit, I'm a pantser. I write by the seat of my pants with no definite outline, making up one tense moment after another. That approach isn't for everyone, but it works for me. I love it when readers say they couldn't put my book down. That's when I know I did something right. I wish my process was more intellectual and captivating, but it is what it is.

What has been your most memorable moment as an author so far?

What comes to mind right away is the day Deception & Consequences went #1 on Ingram in the Romance-Suspense category. I had no idea this had happened, but my publisher texted me and asked me to meet her at a bar downtown. When she walked in, she had a giant poster of my book cover where she had added #1 Bestseller at the top. She just walked in and gave me this look like she was mad and said, "Marcy, Deception & Consequences has been out eleven days, and it became an Ingram romance-suspense bestseller." I was blown away. But what she said next was hilarious. "All I have to say is—what took you so long?"

It was a great day, and she was very wise, presenting that honor to me at a little Irish pub because we celebrated!

> *Deception & Consequences* by Marcy Bialeschki is a thrilling blend of romance, suspense, and family drama. With a strong heroine, sizzling chemistry, and high-stakes tension, the novel captivates readers

What advice would you give to aspiring authors who are just starting out in their writing journey?

Write about what lights you up, and don't worry about everyone else. At one point, I was reading prolifically in my genre and comparing my work with other authors. Consequently, I changed my style to fit a mold, but it wasn't working for me. I was miserable and unsatisfied, and my writing became work.

I met with my publisher, and she gave me the best advice ever: "You'll never please everyone. Just be Marcy, and let your readers find you."

That day I learned my biggest lesson, and I'll share the wisdom: If you just be you, writing will always be your passion and never work. And that's a good life to live. Trust me.

Exploring A Mastermind Of Horror Fiction

MARK ANTHONY

Weaves Dark Magic Through His Award-Winning "LIT" Series

Mark Anthony shares his journey from nurse to award-winning author, details his creative process, and teases the spine-chilling future of the captivating "LIT" series.

"Horror isn't just about fear. For me, it's about emotion, humanity, and the shadows we all carry."

as told to Dan Peters

Mark Anthony's name has become synonymous with dark storytelling that lingers in the minds of readers long after the final page has been turned. An extraordinary talent emerging from Perth, Australia, Anthony has successfully blended his professional career as a compassionate Cancer Nurse with his remarkable gift for crafting haunting narratives. His *Lit* series, born out of a nightmare that sparked an uncontainable creative fire, stands as a testament to both his vivid imagination and his natural aptitude for storytelling.

Since the release of *Lit*—the gripping debut that introduced readers to the unforgettable trio of Ellie, Josh, and Sam, and the chilling shadow people that plague their world—Anthony has cemented his place in the pantheon of modern horror writers. Garnering five-star acclaim from respected platforms such as Goodreads and Kirkus Reviews, each installment in the series has expanded the dark, intricate universe he weaves. His follow-up novels, "*Ascent*" and the recently released *Rage*, delve deeper into the lore, preserving the raw intensity of the original while enriching the narrative with fresh characters and compelling dynamics. It is no wonder his works have earned Gold Literary Titan awards and collective praise from critics and fans alike.

What truly sets Mark Anthony apart is the signature voice he brings to the horror genre—a voice unafraid of exploring life's darkest recesses while anchoring his tales in humanity and profound emotion. His ability to make readers cling to every word and reflect on his stories long after they have ended is a rare gift indeed. Whether he's penning advice on character creation for *Killer Nashville Magazine* or shaping his next masterpiece under the vibrant lights of Barcelona, Anthony continues to redefine and elevate the genre.

In this exclusive interview with *Reader's House*, we sit down with the man who has drawn so many into his macabre yet mesmerising worlds. Join us as Mark Anthony reflects on his journey, his inspirations, and the stories still waiting to be told.

What inspired you to write 'LIT', and how did your personal experiences influence its creation?

It began with a bad dream. One of those nightmares that when you wake, it haunts you for the rest of the day. I built the story, in its most basic form around the premise of that dream. The main character was already there, and the gruesome idea was already in place. Shadow people, the shadow self, all those concepts came into play.

Can you elaborate on the concept of 'Conduits' in 'LIT' and how you developed this unique element?

I found the term for the process, not the process for the term. The exciting thing about it was that the Conduit was simply, a person. An ordinary, everyday person who had to deal with this supernatural, violent intrusion into their lives whilst living in complete isolation and loneliness. The Conduit enabled me to build real, vibrant characters. Each with their own pain, trauma and ways of dealing with this curse. As a writer, it allowed me the freedom to play in the beautiful grey areas of the human condition. That was so much fun. No bad, no good. No guilty, no innocent.

How do you balance the supernatural and psychological aspects in your storytelling to create a compelling narrative?

People can have painful lives. Loss, trauma, depression, fear. I think everyone knows these feelings and these govern an individual's reaction to the supernatural. The series had a lot of attention from ambassadors of Mental Health, and I am grateful for that. The horror aspects show that people will find strength wherever they can. That to hope, is sometimes scary. To care is sometimes risky. Each character in the LIT series fights their own monster and their

Mark Anthony masterfully creates gripping horror tales with unforgettable characters, earning universal acclaim and elevating the genre to new heights.

own trauma. I hope readers can relate to this, as I know I can.

What challenges did you face while writing the 'LIT' series, and how did you overcome them?

I thoroughly enjoyed the whole process! Well, most of it. Writer's block was never really a problem for me however, sinking into the process could be quite challenging because I am quite an upbeat person! I think it's important to just write. Just start and keep going. I knew what I wanted the story to be, so I kept myself on track by focusing on the end goal and pace of a particular storyline. Writing the violence was never fun but necessary. It truly is scary what you can imagine in your own mind. We all do it, its just I make a storyline around it.

How has your background as an avid fan of supernatural and dark fantasy genres shaped your writing style?

It's the greats that inspired me. Peter Blatty, Dean Koontz and Anne Rice. I think because my imagination is very visual, and I always found that great storytelling coupled with amazing and vibrant characters took the story so far. Great visual references and well written characters are essential. The reader must care what the characters are up against! It elevates threat, fear and suspense. The reader walks with the character. If the character resonates with them, the reader will bond with them and follow them with dedication and feeling. The reviews for the series indicate my readers love the characters and feel they can relate with one or more of them. The readers own these characters and invest heavily in them. I have to respect that in my writing.

Could you share insights into your writing process, particularly how you build suspense and tension in your novels?

Picture the scene in your mind. Feel it, see it, smell it and hear it. I create image

Mark Anthony's *LIT* is a dark, gripping fantasy that blends supernatural horror with deep human emotion. Exploring malevolent Leviathans feeding on vulnerable souls, it follows three Conduits navigating trauma, alliances, and terror. With suspenseful prose, profound themes, and compelling characters, *LIT* is an evocative and promising start to the series.

boards and have a set playlist of music for when I am writing. They are all very centric to me. Images that create feeling or spark a mood. A phrase that brings me to that place to write, that atmosphere to work within. Music causes emotions. I use it to bring a certain theme or gravitas to my work as I write. Everyone is different.

What themes do you hope readers will take away from the 'LIT' series?

I am hoping it moves people. Yes, it scares people. It is dark, surreal and at times, even disturbing. But watch the way the people move within it and the relationships that form. It speaks to real people, the reality of no complete good, no complete bad and how innocence can be lost as a reaction to fear.

What advice would you offer to aspiring authors looking to write in the supernatural and dark fantasy genres?

Keep writing and have faith in your work. It sounds easier in theory than in execution, but it is essential. Learn all you can, read all you can but somewhere in that keep your own voice. That's what separates you from others. Fine tune your own unique approach.

Award-winning siblings Matt Barrows and Jessica Barrows Beebe discuss their acclaimed novel, Muddy the Water, highlighting their creative process, newsroom inspirations, sibling dynamics, and advice for aspiring co-authors.

MATT BARROWS JESSICA BEEBE

Behind the Scenes of Muddy the Water

Matt and Jessica Bring Their Crime Thriller Muddy the Water to Life with Unstoppable Creativity

as told to Dan Peters

Matt Barrows And Jessica Barrows Beebe are a formidable sibling duo who have taken the literary world by storm with their debut crime thriller, *Muddy the Water*. A gripping tale of deception, identity, and the complex interplay of truth and lies, their novel has already garnered critical acclaim, winning the prestigious Literary Global Book Award for Debut Fiction. While both come from accomplished careers in journalism, their shared passion for storytelling and their ability to weave vivid narratives have crafted a book that is as thrilling as it is deeply thoughtful.

Matt brings with him over two decades of experience as a sports reporter, covering the San Francisco 49ers, while Jessica's work as a journalist, editor, and TV news producer has taken her from the fast-paced corridors of the White House to the chaotic heart of newsrooms. Together, they've transformed a long-standing idea from Matt's early career into a meticulously crafted story that pulses with tension and intrigue. From the newsroom dynamics to the chilling journey into the mind of an undiagnosed psychopath, their collaboration is a masterclass in blending journalistic precision with creative flair.

In this issue, we had the privilege of sitting down with Matt and Jessica to delve into their creative process, the inspirations behind their unforgettable characters, and, of course, the behind-the-scenes moments that only siblings could bring to such a partnership. Their rich backgrounds, shared sense of humour, and commitment to authenticity shine through every page of *Muddy the Water*. For those who love a crime thriller where fact meets fiction in the most compelling way, this novel is not to be missed.

What inspired you both to collaborate on Muddy the Water, and how did your backgrounds in journalism influence the story?

We both graduated from the University of Virginia four years apart and went into journalism, Matt in newspapers and Jessica in television news. We've known for years that we have similar tastes in books, TV shows and movies. When the pandemic grounded us to a halt and Matt was completely isolated and Jessica was trapped in her house with three teenagers and a loud husband, we needed an outlet for creativity and to regain our sanity.

In 1997 Matt had driven south from Virginia to Hilton Head, SC, to start a job as a reporter for a small newspaper called the Hilton Head Island Packet. It was a spooky night drive to an unfamiliar place. That's when he started thinking: what if he got bumped off and the guy who showed up for work the next day at The Packet was an impostor? After all, he'd been hired over the phone. No one had any idea what he looked like.

That kernel of an idea rattled around in Matt's head for decades. But it never went beyond that until February 2020, when he relayed the rough idea to Jessica during a family dinner. She loved the story outline and suggested the two write the novel together (Matt was lukewarm on the proposal). Soon after, she was on the phone with a coroner from Jasper County, SC, confirming that a dead body can, n fact, travel 75 miles from an inland river to the ocean largely intact. There was no going back and Matt agreed to co-author the crime thriller with his sister.

> Matt and Jessica masterfully blend journalistic expertise with storytelling brilliance, delivering a debut thriller that's both captivating and authentic.

The novel explores themes of identity and deception—how did you approach crafting Ben Broome as such a complex and charismatic character?

We did a deep dive into psychopathy, a personality disorder that involves a lack of empathy, antisocial behavior, and manipulative tendencies. Ben Broome is an undiagnosed psychopath. He does not relish killing but will do what it takes to achieve his goals. If that requires him to become a charming, charismatic colleague in a newsroom, he can become that person. But you don't have to be a psychopath to don a mask and change your personality. In fact, does anyone ever show their true self?

Jessica, as a former journalist and documentarian, how did your experience shape the portrayal of investigative reporting in the novel?

I worked in newsrooms for a lot of my early career. Those newsrooms are tumultuous places – lots of sweat, stress and yelling. We wanted to show those aspects, and also the idea that reporters work very hard for very little but they are proud to bring important truths to their readers.

Matt, you've covered the San Francisco 49ers for over two decades—did your experience in sports journalism influence any aspects of the book's newsroom setting?

No, not really. We make a few references to professional sports but mostly stay away from it (Ben Broome definitely is not a sports guy). I mostly drew from my two years as a news and environment reporter at the Island Packet. It was such a small, intimate, lively newsroom – everyone was crammed together and there were no secrets. You knew exactly what your colleague was working on because he or she was yammering on the phone inches from you. It was my first full-time job, an experience I'll never forget.

The book shifts between the perspectives of a killer, a detective, and a reporter—what were the challenges and rewards of writing from these different viewpoints?

We found that writing a crime thriller from different viewpoints is essential to keeping the readers on their toes. What one character interprets as a clue might be overlooked or played down by another. What one character thinks is a successful day on the job another believes is a total bust. Not only is it captivating to read these different perspectives, but it takes the reader a minute to decipher and think through what is really going on.

The challenge, on the other hand, is making sure the reader knows from whose perspective their current chapter is told. Every chapter in Muddy the Water starts with the perspective – Ben, Grimes or Florence – but readers need to pay attention as they move along through the book.

With Muddy the Water winning the Literary Global Book Award for Debut Fiction, how do you both feel about the reception, and are there plans for a follow-up?

We are very proud to have received the Literary Global Book Award for Debut Fiction. As journalists, we care about solid, accurate writing and we took pains – and interviewed a number of experts – to make sure our novel was grounded in science and facts. It is really gratifying to be recognized for our work.

We have just begun plotting a sequel — stay tuned!

As siblings, were there any fun disagreements or moments of sibling rivalry during the writing process? Or did you find ways to work together seamlessly?

Overall, we worked well together but "seamlessly" is too strong. Our writing process initially worked like this: Jessica wrote the chapters from the perspectives of the two female characters (the detective and the reporter) and Matt wrote the chapters told by the male antagonist (Ben). Then we swapped our work and edited the other.

The initial editing session was long and grueling because the FIRST SENTENCE that Jessica wrote in the whole book included the word "seagull." According to Matt, who is

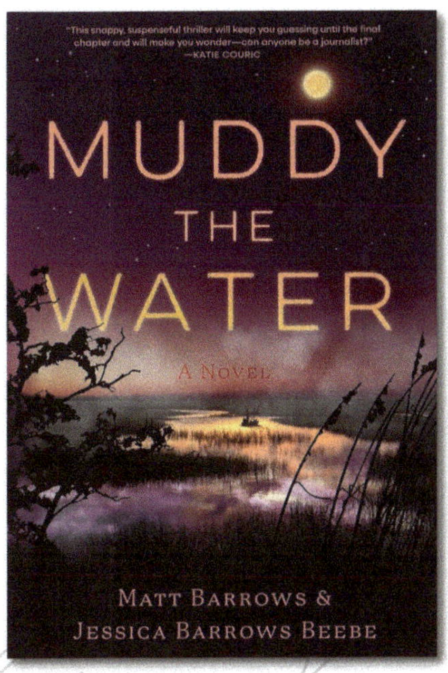

> *Muddy the Water* is an outstanding debut thriller by Matt Barrows and Jessica Barrows Beebe. With a gripping narrative told through three perspectives, the story blends murder, identity, and journalism seamlessly. Character-driven, suspenseful, and fast-paced, it's a masterful exploration of ambition and morality, culminating in a surprising and satisfying finale.

an avid bird watcher, THERE IS NO BIRD CALLED A SEAGULL. He went on to explain in dry, boring terms that the category is "gull" and that there are herring gulls, laughing gulls, ring-billed gulls, etc., etc. Apparently, there are no seagulls. By this point Jessica had put a pillow over her head, knowing it was going to be a bumpy ride to the finish line – five years later.

What advice would you give to aspiring authors looking to co-write a novel, especially those coming from a journalism background?

Set the ground rules for your day-to-day writing life, such as who writes what, who edits what, can someone veto an idea or storyline, who makes research queries? Once the ground rules are set, dive in (and be patient with one another). There are lots of benefits to co-writing a book: it helps ideas flow freely, you presumably can finish faster and potentially double your readership (stay tuned on that last point)!

Oh, and definitely don't use the word "seagull."

Celebrating Diversity, Preserving Heritage, Bridging Cultures

Ritu Hemnani discusses her journey as an author, the influence of family history, writing in verse, cultural preservation, and inspiring younger generations through stories that bridge divides and celebrate shared humanity.

RITU HEMNANI

INSPIRES THROUGH STORIES OF RESILIENCE, IDENTITY, AND CULTURAL HERITAGE

as told to Ben Alan

> "Through my writing, I aim to highlight the hope that can emerge from even the darkest moments."

Ritu Hemnani stands as a beacon of literary brilliance, weaving stories that transcend borders and generations. An author, journalist, and educator, Ritu's work is a testament to the power of storytelling in fostering empathy, preserving heritage, and celebrating diversity. Her historical middle-grade novel in verse, *Lion of the Sky*, published by HarperCollins in 2024, has already captured the hearts of readers with its poignant exploration of migration, resilience, and identity. Looking ahead, her forthcoming narrative non-fiction picture book, *Their Story Is Our Story*, set to be released by Chronicle Books in 2026, promises to further cement her reputation as a masterful storyteller who bridges the past and present with grace and insight.

Ritu's ability to delve into the complexities of human experience, particularly through the lens of her own family's history and cultural heritage, is both moving and inspiring. Her TEDx Talk, *An Inheritance Worth Sharing*, offers a glimpse into the profound personal journey that fuels her creative endeavours, while her contributions to the *South China Morning Post* reflect her commitment to amplifying diverse voices. A British national of Indian descent who calls Hong Kong home, Ritu's multicultural perspective enriches her narratives, making them universally resonant yet deeply rooted in authenticity.

In this exclusive interview, Ritu shares the inspirations

'Lion of the Sky' by Ritu Hemnani is a masterful and heart-wrenching novel in verse that captures the devastating impact of Partition through the eyes of a young boy. With lyrical prose and profound emotion, Hemnani weaves a powerful tale of resilience, identity, and hope that lingers long after the final page.

behind her works, the challenges and rewards of writing in verse, and her hopes for the younger generation. Her words are a call to embrace our shared humanity, honour our roots, and find strength in our stories. It is a privilege to feature such a remarkable voice in this issue of our magazine.

Family history is a recurring theme in your work, particularly in Lion of the Sky. How has your own family's history and cultural heritage influenced your writing journey and the stories you choose to tell?

My family's history, rooted in the trauma of the Partition of India, has profoundly influenced my writing journey. The Partition displaced 14 million people and resulted in over a million deaths, creating a legacy of not just loss and longing but also courage and resilience that resonates deeply within me. This painful history compelled me to explore the emotions tied to migration and uprooting.

As I delved into our family's past, I uncovered stories that many survivors often hesitate to share, revealing both the horrors of displacement and the remarkable bravery of those who endured it. By interviewing elders in my community, I learned about the rich tapestry of life in Hyderabad, Sindh, where diverse faiths coexisted until fear and anger tore them apart. Through my writing, I aim to convey these experiences, highlighting the hope that can emerge from even the darkest moments and emphasizing the importance of belonging and identity in our shared human experience.

Ritu Hemnani is a gifted storyteller whose works illuminate resilience, celebrate diversity, and inspire empathy across generations and cultures.

Writing a verse novel requires a unique balance of narrative and poetic expression. What inspired you to choose this format for Lion of the Sky, and what challenges or rewards did you encounter during the process?

Writing Lion of the Sky as a verse novel allowed me to explore line breaks, punctuation, and rhythm, adding a musical quality that enhances the story. Inspired by how verse novels let readers step into the character's skin, I wanted to use this format to inspire empathy and understanding. Poetic language conveys complex feelings and vivid details, making the characters' pain and strength relatable.

While distilling historical events into concise lines was challenging, the rewards were substantial. The white space creates natural pauses, helping readers absorb the story's importance. This structure is more accessible to reluctant readers, as shorter lines feel less daunting. Additionally, what is left unsaid in a verse novel can be as powerful as the words themselves, allowing for deeper emotional resonance. The visual layout emphasizes key moments and evokes rhythm, drawing readers in.

Your TED Talk about cultural preservation was highly impactful. How has the experience shaped your approach to storytelling, and how do you hope it resonates with younger generations?

My TEDx Talk about cultural preservation significantly shaped my storytelling approach, helping me recognize the importance of sharing diverse narratives. I learned that stories are vital for preserving cultural heritage and collective memories. By incorporating elements of my own background, I aim to help young people connect with their roots and foster empathy for others. I want my stories to resonate with young audiences, inspiring them to embrace their histories and appreciate the various cultures around them. By presenting complex themes in an accessible manner, I hope to spark curiosity and dialogue about identity and belonging. Ultimately, I want young readers to see themselves in these stories, understand the power of their voices, and feel empowered to share their own narratives, contributing to cultural preservation.

With a multicultural upbringing and global experiences, your work bridges cultural divides. How do you approach writing stories that appeal universally while staying true to your cultural roots?

With a multicultural upbringing and global experiences, I focus on universal themes—such as love, loss, and resilience—while honoring my cultural roots. I believe these shared human experiences resonate across cultures, allowing my stories to appeal to a broader audience. I enrich my narratives and celebrate diversity by incorporating specific cultural elements like language, customs, and historical contexts. I create relatable characters who face challenges many can identify with, such as dealing with loss or family expectations, enabling readers from different backgrounds to see themselves in the story. This blend of universal themes and culturally specific details fosters dialogue and connection among diverse audiences, ultimately highlighting the common threads that unite us all.

As someone who has explored various formats and platforms, from novels to TED Talks, what advice would you give to aspiring writers trying to find their unique voice in today's diverse literary landscape?

Aspiring writers should embrace authenticity by drawing from their own experiences and cultural backgrounds, infusing their writing with sincerity and depth. Experimenting with different formats—such as poetry, essays, or multimedia storytelling—can help identify the best way to express ideas and spark innovation. Reading widely across genres and cultures also expands understanding of various narratives and styles, offering inspiration and new perspectives. Engaging with the writing community for feedback enhances growth. By blending authenticity, experimentation, and a dedication to continuous learning, writers can develop a unique voice that resonates powerfully in the literary world.

Inspirational Insights from a Bestselling Author

Susan Weis-Bohlen shares her Ayurvedic journey, writing process, and transformative wellness tips, blending personal experience with ancient wisdom to inspire and empower modern readers.

SUSAN WEIS-BOHLEN

BRINGS ANCIENT AYURVEDIC WISDOM TO MODERN LIVING

as told to Z. Roberts

"My entire lifestyle is Ayurvedic, which can be flexible and forgiving."

Susan Weis-Bohlen is a true luminary in the field of Ayurveda, a revered voice whose work has touched countless lives, guiding people towards balance, healing, and self-discovery. Her profound journey into this ancient Indian science, which began as a personal quest for well-being, has blossomed into a remarkable career as an Ayurvedic consultant, bestselling author, teacher, and retreat leader. Through her books, including *Ayurveda Beginner's Guide: Essential Ayurvedic Principles and Practices to Balance and Heal Naturally, Seasonal Self-Care Rituals: Eat, Breathe, Sleep and Move Better According to Your Dosha,* and *The Beginner's Guide to Ayurvedic Home Remedies: Ancient Healing for Modern Life,* Susan has distilled complex concepts into accessible, practical tools that empower readers to transform their lives.

What makes Susan particularly special is her ability to weave personal experience with timeless Ayurvedic wisdom, creating a connection that resonates deeply with her audience. Her candour about her own life, including her remarkable physical and emotional transformation through Panchakarma, and her insights into overcoming challenges as a writer, serve as a beacon of authenticity and inspiration. Whether she's introducing Ayurvedic principles, sharing simple home remedies, or exploring her own creative process, Susan invites us to live more consciously, joyfully, and in harmony with ourselves and our surroundings.

In addition to her books, Susan's work extends far beyond the page. As the former owner of the cherished Breathe Bookstore Café in Baltimore, a retreat leader who has taken countless participants on journeys to India, Bhutan, and Iceland, and a contributor to respected platforms such as AARP and Llewellyn's publications, she exemplifies a holistic and compassionate approach to life. Her unique perspective on balancing tradition with modernity has made her a trusted guide for those navigating the complexities of contemporary wellness.

We are thrilled to feature Susan Weis-Bohlen in this issue of Reader's House as she reflects on her personal story, professional achievements, and the wisdom that defines her work. Whether you're new to Ayurveda, a seasoned practitioner, or simply curious about holistic living, Susan's insights are bound to leave you enlightened and inspired. Let her words be your guide to taking the first—or next—steps in your own journey to health and self-transformation.

What initially drew you to Ayurveda, and how has it transformed your personal and professional life?

When I was 41 years old, in 2004, I opened a new-age bookstore in Baltimore, Maryland called Breathe Books. I had a small Ayurvedic section, but I didn't know much about it beyond what I had read a decade earlier in Deepak Chopra's book Ageless Body, Timeless Mind. I was drawn to this 5000-year-old Indian science of health and wellbeing because I wanted to lose weight. It turns out, it wasn't about weight, it was about finding balance in my mind, body and spirit.

I discovered there are three doshas – Vata which is air and space, and Pitta, which is fire and water, and Kapha, water and earth. At 230 pounds (16.5 stone), I had excess Kapha. I began studying how to reduce Kapha through food, lifestyle, and more, which led me to the Chopra Center in California for a 10-day program called Panchakarma (PK). The protocol includes oil massages, herbal treatments, and classes in Ayurveda, yoga, and meditation and eating a diet to balance your dosha.

I rapidly dropped 60 pounds (4.2 stone) – never to be seen again, and totally embraced the lifestyle, so much so that I became a certified practitioner through The Chopra Center. I also studied with The Ayurvedic Institute in the US and India for clinical knowledge and with Amadea Morningstar for cooking. From 2019-2023, I was on the board of the

Susan Weis-Bohlen is a gifted healer, storyteller, and teacher whose warmth, authenticity, and expertise make holistic wellness accessible to all.

National Ayurvedic Medical Association (NAMA).

After running my bookstore for 10 years (and adding an Ayurvedic café), I decided to close shop and become a full-time practitioner, teacher, speaker, and author.

Can you share some simple Ayurvedic home remedies that beginners can incorporate into their daily routines?

Eat three meals a day, each meal consisting of about two handfuls of food. Avoid snacks. Have a light dinner, at least three hours before bed. Get to bed around 10 pm so that your body can go through the metabolic process that happens between 10 pm and 2 am (waste is separated from nutrients). This ensures that your body eliminates toxins, rebuilds tissue, cleanses blood and clears the mind. One should wake up around 6 or 7 (depending on the season, your dosha, state of health) feeling rested and ready to go.

Boost your immune system when needed with herbs such as the adaptogen ashwagadha (one or two tablets in the morning for energy OR at night for relaxation.) Keep your colon toned and bowel movements regular with triphala (one or two tablets before bed). The daily oil application called abhyanga keeps the skin supple and blocks environmental toxins.

How did your experience with Panchakarma influence your approach to wellness and self-care?

PK cleanses you inside and out, requires you to rest and allow yourself to be taken care of. In India, I went to Vaidyagrama, Coimbatore, Tamil Nadu, for a three-week PK. I took time to journal, meditate, do some chanting, and listen to nourishing music and podcasts. My husband and I did this together, and it brought us even closer. I try to carry on some techniques at home.

What challenges did you face while writing your books, and how did you overcome them?

I love writing. I've been writing since I was a kid, and I was a journalist in Israel for many years. I didn't set out to write books, but I was contacted by a publisher and decided to go for it. The challenge was that I couldn't see the big picture and would get stuck trying to figure out the structure, the flow, and the end game. I learned from my editors that I didn't need to know everything from the get-go. A table of contents could help guide me, and my natural voice was key.

At first, I thought I should be more clinical, just the facts kind of thing. However, an editor at Simon & Schuster told me that the text "sang" when I included personal stories and asked me for more of that. People can relate to my experiences, see themselves, and connect. I love that. That led to studying creative writing. Currently, I'm working on a memoir, and I lead workshops and trips where we incorporate writing.

I also learned – and this is super important – to read your work out loud. When you hear how it sounds, it begins to make much more sense, and corrections are evident. You can read it to a person, to your dogs, or into a voice recorder and listen back – but you MUST include this step in the writing process.

And revise, revise, revise. First, I just have to get the story out onto the page. Then, I let it sit and marinate, return to it a few days or weeks later, and begin the layering process. Who was I then? Who am I now? What did I learn? Am I using all my senses to tell the story? What did I see? What did it smell like, the colors, foods, weather, etc. I steep myself in the story and try to bring it to life, moment by moment, so that the reader can experience it too.

What was the most surprising discovery you made during your studies of Ayurveda?

It's a rare thing for someone to lose as much weight as I did and never gain it back, but I learned from Ayurveda that I wasn't fat just because I ate too much. I was fat because it was in my natural doshic makeup to hold on - emotional baggage, people, things, routines. As I became more balanced, physically and emotionally, the weight fell off. I didn't need it anymore. My new book will go into this in detail, but it was fascinating.

How do you balance your writing, teaching, and personal life while staying true to your Ayurvedic practices?

After nearly 20 years of practice, the benefits are

Ayurveda Beginner's Guide by Susan Weis-Bohlen is an approachable introduction to Ayurveda, offering clear explanations of doshas, practical lifestyle tips, and a gentle three-week plan. Perfect for beginners, it provides recipes, yoga, and meditation guidance. While introductory in scope, it's a valuable resource for starting a balanced, Ayurvedic journey.

so clear, and our lives are so rich because of it. Our entire lifestyle is Ayurvedic, which can be flexible and forgiving. Do we take pharmaceuticals from time to time? Yes, when necessary. Do we eat ice cream in winter sometimes? Yes – I call it vitamin H – Vitamin Happy. And as I've gone through menopause, I could not mitigate some of my symptoms Ayurvedically (although some people are able to) and I began using estrogen and progesterone and I'm cool with that.

My writing practice is truly Ayurvedic. I wish I was one of those people who write at 5 in the morning, when the world is still and the house quiet, but as a true Kapha, I'm asleep at 5 and you literally couldn't pay me to write then! I discovered that my best work happens between 2 pm and 6 pm, which is Vata time day. Vata dosha is highly creative, so there ya go! Creativity flows for me in the afternoon, so that's my process. My writing space and the direction my desk faces are based on Vastu Shastra, which is Vedic Feng Shui. Our entire house is Vastu'ed which helps to keep us balanced and healthy.

What advice would you give to aspiring authors who want to write about holistic health and wellness?

You must be authentic and, ideally, have healed yourself through the practice you are writing about. Come from a place of vulnerability, not victimhood. Show your weaknesses and how they became your strengths. Give credit to your teachers. Be open and honest, warm and encouraging. And read. You must be a reader to be a writer. Notice how the books you love are structured. Go to events or retreats with your favorite teachers and listen closely to them. Be discerning. And be original. We all have a story to tell.

A Journey Through Southern Culture, Strong Female Characters, And The Art Of Storytelling

KAREN WHITE

UNVEILS THE SECRETS BEHIND HER BESTSELLING NOVELS

as told to Dan Peters

Karen White shares insights on her Southern roots, writing process, character development, and upcoming works in this in-depth interview.

Karen White, a luminous beacon in the world of contemporary fiction, has captivated readers with her richly woven narratives and unforgettable characters. With nearly two million books in print, translated into fifteen languages, and a succession of bestsellers on both the New York Times and USA Today lists, her acclaim is well-deserved.

A master storyteller with a unique ability to blend family drama, mystery, and romance, Karen draws upon her deeply Southern roots, crafting tales that resonate with authenticity and emotion. Her novels, often set against the backdrop of the South, reflect a profound understanding of the region's rich culture and complex characters. From the hauntingly beautiful landscapes of New Orleans to the historic charm of Charleston, Karen's settings are not merely backdrops but living entities that shape her narratives.

Her latest works, including the celebrated The Lost Summers of Newport and the new The House on Prytania, showcase her skill in creating multi-dimensional stories that explore the intricacies of human relationships and the enduring power of love. Karen's upcoming novel, That Last Carolina Summer, scheduled for release in July 2025, is another testament to her prolific writing journey that continues to inspire and entertain.

In this issue of Reader's House magazine, we delve into an enlightening conversation with Karen White, exploring her transition from the business world to becoming a bestselling author, her creative process, and the personal experiences that fuel her narratives. It is a privilege to bring you closer to one of today's most beloved authors, whose dedication to her craft and passion for storytelling leaves an indelible mark on readers everywhere.

What inspired you to set many of your novels in the South, and how does the region influence your storytelling?

My family has been in the South since before the American Revolution, so my roots grow deep in this region. Both of my parents were born and raised in Mississippi and my summers were spent visiting

Continued *on page 42*

"Karen White, bestselling author and master storyteller, shares her passion for writing and the deep Southern roots that inspire her captivating narratives."

Continued from page 40

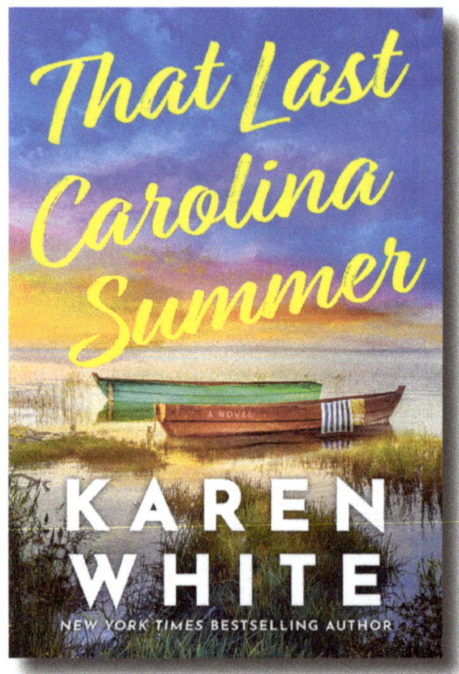

In *That Last Carolina Summer,* Karen White explores sisterhood and secrets through Phoebe Manigault's return to Charleston, where family tensions and haunting memories resurface. The novel beautifully intertwines themes of grief and redemption against the evocative Southern backdrop, culminating in a profound and emotional journey.

grandparents and cousins regardless of where in the world we lived. Although I never lived in the South until after I was married, I always considered myself Southern. There is something poetic about the way people talk and the way they tell their stories. Even the oppressive heat of a July afternoon spent on my grandmother's porch became a cornerstone of my childhood memories and part of what I attempt to recreate in my novels.

How did your experience growing up in a house full of brothers shape the strong female characters in your books?

I learned early on that my brothers would always be stronger and taller than I was, and I was destined to be on the losing end of any snowball fight or any other feats of strength. I spent a lot of my younger years hiding from my brothers while they chased me with a large insect or reptile. That's when I discovered the immersive world of books and the power of words that were my only weapons against my brothers. But it is my maternal grandmother who raised six children while running her own business despite having only a third grade education that inspired my strong and resilient protagonists.

Can you share the story behind your transition from a career in business to becoming a bestselling author?

I left my job as an operations manager for a software development company when my first daughter was born and we moved to Atlanta. In between feedings and diaper changes, I rediscovered my love for books which had been mostly dormant since I'd finished college. I'd never planned to be a writer, but after binge-reading Diana Gabaldon's Outlander series, I had a book hangover and couldn't read another book. So I did what my teachers had always said I should do and wrote my first book. I entered it into a contest and ended up not only winning but also garnered an offer for representation by a New York literary agent who sold that book and the next nine. I kept writing and selling books and it was only after twelve or so books that I realized that perhaps this writing thing wasn't a fluke and just maybe I was meant to be a writer after all.

What was the most challenging part of writing your first novel, In the Shadow of the Moon, and how did you overcome it?

Time! With two young children and a husband who traveled most days for work, I had to be really efficient at time organization. It's true, however, that the busier a person is, the better they are at time management. As an empty-nester now, I find it much hard to manage my time—something for which I blame social media. It can be entertaining and helpful, but most of the time but I find that it takes up a lot of my time.

The Tradd Street series is beloved by many readers. What inspired you to create this Charleston-set mystery series?

I cut my reading teeth on the Nancy Drew mystery series so it was probably inevitable that once I turned to writing, creating a female-centered series with a paranormal bent would be a natural progression in my career.

How do you balance elements of family drama, mystery, intrigue, and romance in your novels to create such compelling stories?

My goal since writing my very first novel is to create the sort of book with the same kind of elements that I enjoy in the books I read: multi-layered stories with multiple interwoven elements. That creates multi-dimensional books that are enjoyable not just to read, but to also to write.

> *"My family has been in the South since before the American Revolution, so my roots grow deep in this region."*

What advice would you give to aspiring authors who are hesitant to take the leap into writing?

Read, read, read--across all genres. Then, to borrow from Nike, just do it. Write. Don't worry if you're doing it the right way (there is no right way), and quiet all the voices in your head and just write. It won't be perfect, but as long as you have words on the page, you can fix them later.

Can you tell us about your writing process and how you develop intricate plotlines and memorable characters?

I'm a terrible example to new writers! I don't prewrite or do character sketches or write an outline. I start with my protagonist and setting (which is always a primary character in my novels) and the protagonist's internal and external conflicts and just start writing. I see the story unfold from my protagonist's viewpoint and I just write it down. And, no, I rarely know the ending when I

"My goal since writing my very first novel is to create the sort of book with the same kind of elements that I enjoy in the books I read: multi-layered stories with multiple interwoven elements."

start.

What advice would you give to aspiring writers who are struggling to find their unique voice or style?

Just keep writing until it clicks and you know you're on the right path. It's like being proficient on an instrument or sport: it takes practice.

What has been the most rewarding part of your writing journey, and how do you stay inspired to keep creating new stories?

My favorite part of writing is typing THE END. My second is hearing from readers. It's humbling when I learn that my writing has inspired or comforted, and thrilling when they talk about my characters as if they're as real in their heads as they are in mine.

KAREN WHITE

With almost two million books in print in fifteen different languages, Karen White is a New York Times and USA Today bestselling author of 34 novels.

Raised in a house full of brothers, Karen's love of books and strong female characters first began in the third grade when the local librarian placed The Secret of the Old Clock, a Nancy Drew Mystery, in her hands.

Although most of her growing up years were spent in London, England, Karen's roots run deep in the South where many of her novels are set. Her intricate plot lines and compelling characters charm and captivate readers with just the right mix of family drama, mystery, intrigue and romance.

Not entirely convinced she wanted to be a writer, Karen first pursued a career in business and graduated cum laude with a BS in Management from Tulane University. Ten years later, in a weak moment, she wrote her first book. In the Shadow of the Moon was published in August, 2000. Her books—referred to as "grit lit" (Southern Women's Fiction)—have since been nominated for numerous national contests including the SIBA (Southeastern Booksellers Alliance) Fiction Book of the Year.

Karen's latest releases include The House on Prytania (May 2023) and the instant New York Times bestseller, The Lost Summers of Newport (May 2022), a collaboration with authors Beatriz Williams and Lauren Willig. The House on Prytania is the first book in a new series set in New Orleans and starring Nola Trenholm from the popular Charleston-set Tradd Street series.

Next up for fans of Karen White is That Last Carolina Summer, scheduled for publication by Park Row Books, an imprint of HarperCollins Publishers, in July, 2025.

When not writing, Karen spends her time reading, singing, and avoiding cooking. Karen and her husband have two grown children and a spoiled Havanese dog, Sophie, and divides her time between Atlanta, Georgia and the northwest Florida coast.

Award-winning writer T. R. Hamby shares insights into her creative process, her love for character-driven storytelling, and the inspiration behind her multi-genre successes, including Stages and King of the Wicked.

T. R. Hamby Explores Her Literary Journey That Made Her A Fan-Favourite Author

Creative Inspiration, Compelling Characters, And The Power Of Storytelling

T. R. Hamby is an author whose talent and passion for storytelling have earned her a distinctive place in the literary world. With an astounding fifteen books independently published since 2021, she has demonstrated an unwavering dedication to her craft, captivating readers across an impressive range of genres, from fantasy and psychological thrillers to heartfelt LGBTQ stories. Hamby's characters are brimming with life, her plots are daringly original, and her ability to weave complex emotions into her narratives is second to none. Whether exploring themes of self-discovery in *Stages* or reimagining mythological beings in *King of the Wicked*, Hamby's works possess a depth that resonates with readers long after the final page.

> **T. R. Hamby's** *compelling storytelling, vivid imagination, and emotional depth make her an exceptional, one-of-a-kind talent who captivates readers with her profound and daring narratives.*

It is little surprise that Hamby's journey as a writer began early, with story-filled notebooks and a relentless imagination driving her forward. Her stories—brilliantly character-driven and often sparked by personal inspiration—have struck a chord with countless fans. In this interview, we gain a rare glimpse into the mind behind the magic. With a refreshingly candid take on her influences, process, and the characters she holds dear, Hamby reminds us why she has swiftly become a beloved voice in contemporary fiction. For both aspiring writers and devoted readers, this conversation offers a wealth of insight into the art and heart of storytelling. Enjoy!

What inspired you to start writing novels at such a young age, and how has your writing process evolved over the years?

I have always been an avid storyteller. Even before I could write I was telling stories, sometimes with my dolls and sometimes with my drawings. I've always had a flair for drama, and found great inspiration in both movies and books.

When I was in school I would write my stories in spiral-bound notebooks. I'd carry them with me everywhere and write when I had a free moment. I write by the seat of my pants, meaning I just have to take off writing to get a story out, no outline, so you can imagine those first stories were lengthy! These days I have more structure and limits, but my process has always been figuring it out as I go along, especially letting the characters tell the story.

Your books span multiple genres, from fantasy to psychological thrillers and LGBTQ stories. How do you decide which genre to write next?

It's usually my characters that dictate what kind of a story I'll be writing next. I'll think up a character, their looks and their behavior, and this will coax out the type of story and its style. My characters are always guiding the story! But I also find inspiration in books and movies. Give me a good horror film or a sweeping fantasy novel and I'll think, "I should write something like that."

Stages explores themes of self-discovery and identity—what inspired Billy's journey, and how did you approach writing such a personal and emotional story?

Billy is a very special character for me. He sprung up while I was working on a different project and wouldn't let me go. His need to explore who he is while also handling what others expect from him is something I think most people can relate to. There are many people like Billy, trying to find their places in the world, all of whom have inspired and continue to inspire me.

I tried to be as open and honest in my writing with this story. As I do with every story, I let my characters tell it. Billy has a strong voice, even if he is unsure of himself at times. He helped me navigate his story with grace.

King of the Wicked presents a fresh take on angels and mythology. What research or influences shaped your version of these legendary beings?

I took a lot of inspiration from biblical lore. I grew up learning about St. Michael the archangel casting Satan out of Hell, and I got to wondering about it. If Michael and Lucifer were both angels in Heaven at one point, were they once friends? And the inspiration started there. I strove to make the angels as divine as possible while also making them as fallible as humans.

Many writers develop deep connections with their characters. Which character from your books do you relate to the most, and why?

I find a little bit of myself in most of my characters! But I do find myself reflected in Nora Rossi, the heroine in King of the Wicked. A human who falls in love with an angel, Nora often has to rely on her smarts to navigate the adventurous life she embarks on. She's headstrong and feisty, and doesn't back down easily, all traits I admire. I would say I relate to her most only because I strive to be like her every day.

What advice would you give to aspiring writers who want to publish their own stories?

Never stop writing, even when you think no one would ever read it. Sometimes you have to crank out some bad work in order to produce something good. The more you write, the better you'll get, and the more you'll learn.

Terence Hannum discusses The interplay of life, decay technology

A Journey Through Nature's Shadows

Terence Hannum explores psychoactive plants in his sculptures, discussing mortality, technology the uncanny, blending art and nature into immersive experiences.

Renowned for his evocative exploration of the intersection between nature and existence, Terence Hannum's artistic practice seamlessly blends the realms of sculpture, painting technology. With an innovative approach that employs 3D modelling and printing, Hannum's work vividly captures the essence of psychoactive and poisonous plants, inviting viewers to ponder themes of mortality, transformation the uncanny. His installations are not merely static displays but living entities that infiltrate and interact with their surroundings, creating immersive environments that challenge our perceptions of life and decay.

Hannum delves into the inspirations behind his thought-provoking sculptures and the creative processes that inform his unique installations. He reflects on how science fiction influences his artistic vision and the ways in which he manipulates materials and lighting to evoke an otherworldly quality in his work. Join us as we explore the mind of an artist who is reshaping our understanding of botanical forms and their implications for existence, inviting us to confront the delicate balance between beauty and decay.

What inspired you both to collaborate on Muddy the Water, and how did your backgrounds in journalism influence the story?

We both graduated from the University of Virginia four years apart and went into journalism, Matt in newspapers and Jessica in television news. We've known for years that we have similar tastes in books, TV shows and movies. When the pandemic grounded us to a halt and Matt was completely isolated and Jessica was trapped in her house with three teenagers and a loud husband, we needed an outlet for creativity and to regain our sanity.

In 1997 Matt had driven south from Virginia to Hilton Head, SC, to start a job as a reporter for a small newspaper called the Hilton Head Island Packet. It was a spooky night drive to an unfamiliar place. That's when he started thinking: what if he got bumped off and the guy who showed up for work the next day at The Packet was an impostor? After all, he'd been hired over the phone. No one had any idea what he looked like.

That kernel of an idea rattled around in Matt's head for decades. But it never went beyond that until February 2020, when he relayed the rough idea to Jessica during a family dinner. She loved the story outline and suggested the two write the novel together (Matt was lukewarm on the proposal). Soon after, she was on the phone with a coroner from Jasper County, SC, confirming that a dead body can, in fact, travel 75 miles from an inland river to the ocean largely intact. There was no going back and Matt agreed to co-author the crime thriller with his sister.

The novel explores themes of identity and deception—how did you approach crafting Ben Broome as such a complex and charismatic character?

We did a deep dive into psychopathy, a personality disorder that involves a lack of empathy, antisocial behavior, and manipulative tendencies. Ben Broome is an undiagnosed psychopath. He does not relish killing but will do what it takes to achieve his goals. If that requires him to become a charming, charismatic colleague in a newsroom, he can become that person. But you don't have to be a psychopath to don a mask and change your personality. In fact, does anyone ever show their true self?

Jessica, as a former journalist and documentarian, how did your experience shape the portrayal of investigative reporting in the novel?

I worked in newsrooms for a lot of my early career. Those newsrooms are tumultuous places – lots of sweat, stress and yelling. We wanted to show those aspects, and also the idea that reporters work very hard for very little but they are proud to bring important truths to their readers.

Matt, you've covered the San Francisco 49ers for over two decades—did your experience in sports journalism influence any aspects of the book's newsroom setting?

No, not really. We make a few references to professional sports but mostly stay away from it (Ben Broome definitely is not a sports guy). I mostly drew from my two years as a news and environment reporter at the Island Packet. It was such a small, intimate, lively newsroom – everyone was crammed together and there were no secrets. You knew exactly what your colleague was working on because he or she was yammering on the phone inches from you. It was my first full-time job, an experience I'll never forget.

The book shifts between the perspectives of a killer, a detective, and a reporter—what were the challenges and rewards of writing from these different viewpoints?

We found that writing a crime thriller from different viewpoints is essential to keeping the readers on their toes. What one character interprets as a clue might be overlooked or played down by another. What one character thinks is a successful day on the job another believes is a total bust. Not only is it captivating to read these different perspectives, but it takes the reader a minute to decipher and think through what is really going on.

The challenge, on the other hand, is making sure the reader knows from whose perspective their current chapter is told. Every chapter in Muddy the Water starts with the perspective – Ben, Grimes or Florence – but readers need to pay attention as they move along through the book.

With Muddy the Water winning the Literary Global Book Award for Debut Fiction, how do you both feel about the reception, and are there plans for a follow-up?

We are very proud to have received the Literary Global Book Award for Debut Fiction. As journalists, we care about solid, accurate writing and we took pains – and interviewed a number of experts – to make sure our novel was grounded in science and facts. It is really gratifying to be recognized for our work.

The Impact of Historical Storytelling on Future Generations

Dr. Walter B. Curry, Jr. discusses his passion for uncovering hidden histories, research challenges, and the transformative impact of historical storytelling, while inspiring future authors with invaluable advice.

WALTER B. CURRY JR

SHARES THE POWER OF STORYTELLING IN PRESERVING AFRICAN AMERICAN HISTORY

"I aimed to illuminate our shared history and preserve the family legacy by highlighting overlooked contributions to African American history."

as told to Ben Alan

Dr. Walter B. Curry, Jr. stands as a powerful voice in the rich tapestry of historical and genealogical literature, weaving compelling narratives that resonate deeply with readers and scholars alike. A native of Orangeburg, South Carolina, Dr. Curry has made it his life's mission to shine a light on the often-overlooked chapters of African American history through the lens of family heritage and community. His literary contributions are nothing short of remarkable, with each work serving as both a deeply personal testament and an invaluable historical record.

As the founder of Renaissance Publications, LLC, Dr. Curry has set a high bar in the literary arts, producing award-winning books such as *"The Thompson Family: Untold Stories from the Past (1830-1960)"* and *"The Awakening: The Seawright-Ellison Family Saga, Vol. 1, A Narrative History."* These works delve into stories of resilience, triumph, and transformation, tracing the lives of his ancestors through pivotal moments in American history, from slavery to Reconstruction and beyond. His most recent achievement, *"South Carolina Matilda Evans: A Medical Pioneer,"* further underscores his unparalleled ability to bring historical figures to life. By chronicling the legacy of Dr. Matilda Evans—the trailblazing physician who became the first African American woman licensed to practise medicine in South Carolina—he has once again illuminated a path for future generations to follow.

Dr. Curry's dedication extends beyond the written word. As the Author-In-Residence at the Aiken Center for the Arts, he transforms historical narratives into engaging educational experiences, fostering a love for storytelling among young minds. Whether conducting local workshops, presenting at conferences, or guiding students through history using innovative techniques, he exemplifies a passion for learning and community enrichment. It is no surprise that his work has earned him countless accolades, cementing his reputation as a visionary scholar, storyteller, and educator.

Reader's House magazine is proud to present an exclusive interview with this extraordinary author. In the conversation that follows, Dr. Curry not only shares insights into the intricate process of unearthing hidden histories but also offers invaluable guidance to aspiring writers. His journey is a testament to the transformative power of storytelling, and it is a privilege to showcase his voice within these pages.

What inspired you to write about the Seawright-Ellison family and their journey through such pivotal moments in American history?

The motivation behind writing about the Seawright-Ellison family stems from a desire to illuminate the shared history of two families linked by their common ancestor, Martha Kitchings Seawright Ellison, who was born into slavery in 1849 in Aiken County, South Carolina. This narrative chronicles the family's journey through significant historical events, including Martha's experiences during slavery, the Civil War, and the Reconstruction Era, as well as their life in Aiken County and beyond. Additionally, I aimed to preserve the family legacy by bringing to light the stories of relatives who have been overlooked over time, highlighting their contributions to African American history in Aiken County and beyond.

> Dr. Curry masterfully preserves overlooked histories, blending meticulous research with storytelling to inspire understanding, pride, and community connection.

Can you share some insights into your research process for uncovering the untold stories of the Thompson family?

The research process I employed to uncover the untold stories of the Thompson family involved a blend of oral and written narratives. Oral narratives were gathered through interviews and informal discussions with both relatives and acquaintances who had recollections of the individuals and events associated with the Thompson family. In addition, written narratives were sourced from newspaper articles, property deeds, photographs, and other primary documents.

What challenges did you face while compiling historical narratives, and how did you overcome them?

When putting together stories from the past, I encountered several difficulties that made the process quite challenging. One major issue was finding reliable sources of information, as some historical accounts can be biased or incomplete. To tackle this, I made sure to cross-check facts from multiple sources, like books, articles, and interviews with experts. Another challenge was organizing the information in a way that made sense and flowed well for the reader. I overcame this by creating outlines and using timelines to help me visualize the sequence of events. Additionally, I sometimes struggled with making the narratives engaging and relatable to my audience. To fix this, I focused on including interesting details and personal stories that would capture the reader's attention and make the history feel alive.

How do you think Dr. Matilda Evans' contributions to healthcare have influenced modern medical practices in South Carolina?

Dr. Matilda Evans made a significant impact by offering medical care to people who couldn't pay for high-quality healthcare. Her dedication to helping those in need is truly remarkable, as she worked tirelessly to ensure that everyone, regardless of their financial situation, had access to the medical services they required. Through her efforts, she not only improved the health of many individuals but also inspired others to think about the importance of providing care to underserved communities. Dr. Evans' legacy continues to remind us of the vital role that compassion and commitment play in the field of medicine.

As an Author-In-Residence at the Aiken Center for the Arts, how do you engage students with historical storytelling?

As an Author-In-Residence at the Aiken Center for the Arts, I find creative ways to connect with students through the art of historical storytelling. I believe that history comes alive when we share it in an engaging manner, so I often use interactive activities, like role-playing or group discussions, to help students immerse themselves in the stories of the past. By encouraging them to think critically about historical events and the people involved, I aim to spark their imagination and make them feel like they are part of the narrative. This approach not only makes learning fun but also helps students understand the importance of history in shaping our world today.

What advice would you give to aspiring authors interested in writing historical and genealogical narratives?

If you want to write historical and genealogical stories, my best advice is to start by doing a lot of research. Look into the time periods and events you want to write about, and try to find interesting facts that can make your story come alive. It's also really helpful to talk to family members or look through old documents to gather personal stories that can add depth to your writing. Don't forget to pay attention to the details, like the way people dressed or the kinds of food they ate, because these little things can make your narrative feel more authentic. Lastly, keep writing and revising your work, because practice is key to becoming a better author.

> Dr. Walter B. Curry Jr.'s 'The Thompson Family: Untold Stories From The Past (1830-1960)' is a moving, richly detailed account of resilience and triumph. This award-winning masterpiece connects personal genealogy to profound historical events, offering an inspiring look at an African American family's legacy. A must-read for history enthusiasts and genealogists alike!

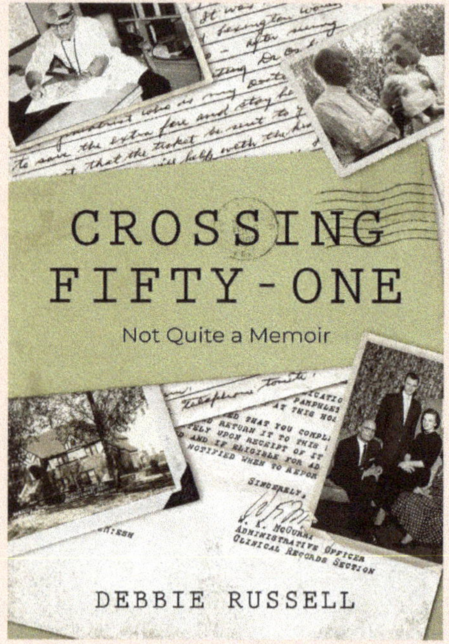

CROSSING FIFTY-ONE

by Debbie Russell

A deeply moving, beautifully written memoir blending mystery, family secrets, and resilience, Crossing Fifty-One is a must-read emotional journey.

Debbie Russell's *Crossing Fifty-One* is a deeply introspective, multi-generational exploration of family, addiction, identity, and personal reinvention. As a former trial lawyer, Russell turns her investigative instincts inward, embarking on a journey through her family's past that is as revealing as it is emotionally raw. The memoir—though structured like a mystery—examines how secrets, grief, and resilience shape the lives of generations.

At the heart of the book is Russell's relationship with her father, a man she deeply admires, yet one whose history is intertwined with hidden truths. When he enters hospice care, Russell finds herself confronting long-suppressed family dynamics. Her search for answers leads her to her grandfather, Dr. Ralph Russell, who voluntarily admitted himself into a federal drug-treatment facility in 1951. Through archival letters and relentless research, she pieces together his battle with addiction and its reverberations through her lineage.

The memoir beautifully balances the intellectual rigor of a legal mind with the vulnerability of a daughter trying to make peace with her past. Russell's writing is gripping, sometimes heart-wrenching, yet infused with hope. Her reflections on midlife crisis, grief, and self-discovery resonate universally, making this book a compelling read for those navigating their own familial complexities.

Crossing Fifty-One is not just a memoir—it is an invitation to examine our own histories, to seek understanding amid pain, and to redefine ourselves beyond the roles we inherit. A powerful and thought-provoking debut.

CRUSADER'S PATH

by Mary Ann Bernal

A beautifully written, historically rich novel that masterfully blends faith, love, and redemption against the gripping backdrop of the First Crusade.

Mary Ann Bernal's *Crusader's Path* is a deeply moving and historically rich novel that transports readers to the turbulent era of the First Crusade. With a keen eye for detail and a talent for blending history with human emotion, Bernal crafts a compelling narrative of faith, redemption, and love against the backdrop of war and religious fervor.

The novel follows Etienne, a knight driven by a quest for redemption, and Avielle, a woman profoundly impacted by religious devotion and the horrors of conflict. Their paths cross in Constantinople, where shared trauma and a fragile hope bind them together. Bernal masterfully develops their relationship, weaving a love story that feels both authentic and heartbreaking. Etienne's internal struggle between his sacred vow and his love for Avielle adds emotional depth, making his journey profoundly relatable.

What sets *Crusader's Path* apart is Bernal's commitment to historical accuracy. The vivid descriptions of medieval Europe, the brutal realities of war, and the religious fervor of the time create an immersive reading experience. Her portrayal of the characters is nuanced—no one is purely heroic or villainous, reflecting the moral complexities of the Crusades.

With beautifully crafted prose, gripping historical insight, and a powerful exploration of faith and love, *Crusader's Path* is a must-read for historical fiction enthusiasts. Bernal delivers a poignant tale that lingers long after the final page, making this novel a standout in the genre.

BLUE BY YOU

by Larry B. Gildersleeve

A beautifully written, heartfelt journey of love, loss, and redemption, Blue by You masterfully explores the power of second chances.

Larry B. Gildersleeve's *Blue by You* is an emotionally evocative exploration of love, loss, and second chances that will resonate deeply with fans of introspective and character-driven storytelling. The novel opens with Daniel, a man consumed by grief after losing his young wife to cancer. Retreating to the solitude of the Colorado mountains with only his loyal dog, Blue, as a companion, Daniel embodies the fragility of a man disconnected from purpose. Gildersleeve's vivid descriptions of the serene, yet isolating, mountain backdrop mirror Daniel's inner desolation perfectly.

What sets *Blue by You* apart is the arrival of Paula, a vibrant force who disrupts Daniel's self-imposed exile for one transformative week. Their brief connection is beautifully portrayed, rich with tension, vulnerability, and a hint of magic. Decades later, when fate conspires to reunite them, their unexpected second chance adds a heartwarming twist. However, Paula's inability to recall their earlier encounter introduces layers of mystery and emotional complexity, leaving readers questioning the nature of memory and love.

Gildersleeve's prose is lyrical and poignant, drawing readers into Daniel's perspective with authentic emotion. While the pacing occasionally drags—particularly during the middle sections—the sheer beauty of the writing and the heartfelt storyline compensate for these moments.

Blue by You is a bittersweet, uplifting tale about finding meaning amidst despair and the redemptive power of human connection. Readers searching for a deeply reflective and tender novel will appreciate this gem. Highly recommended.

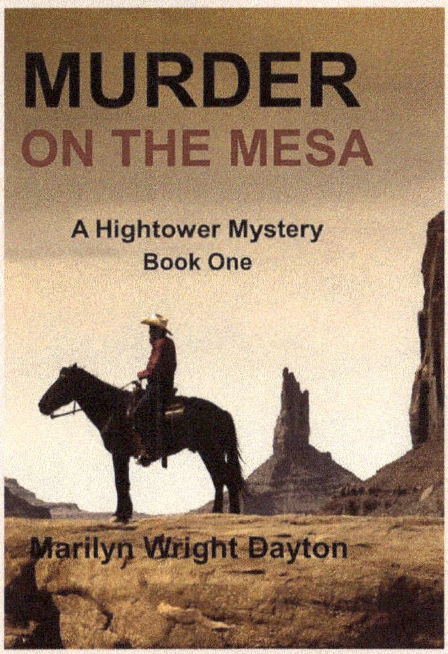

ENIGMA TRACER

by Charles Breakfield and Rox Burkey

An electrifying mix of tech intrigue, action, and suspense; "Enigma Tracer" captivates with compelling characters and an unpredictable plot.

Enigma Tracer: Enigma Heirs - Book 1" is a thrilling dive into the world of high-stakes cyber warfare, corporate greed, and clandestine operations. Charles Breakfield and Rox Burkey have delivered a richly layered narrative that holds readers captive from start to finish. With its blend of tech intrigue, mystery, and action, this book sets a strong foundation for the Enigma Heirs series.

The story revolves around Gracie and her leadership of the R-Group, a family-driven team dedicated to thwarting the nefarious schemes of Phillip Pliant—a brilliant but corrupt CEO of Pliant Industries. Pliant's intricate network, ranging from cartel connections to his revolutionary (and dangerous) 3D-building materials, presents a formidable challenge. The stakes are raised with the introduction of JJ's Cyber Assassin Technology Services (CATS), whose cutting-edge analysis and covert operations elevate the suspense.

The authors expertly weave complex characters with relatable struggles, placing Gracie at the heart of a mission that tests intelligence, loyalty, and courage. The stakes of island survival, corporate sabotage, and the looming threat of chaos keep the tension electrifyingly high throughout. Breakfield and Burkey's attention to detail—especially in the tech and crime domains—makes the plot intriguing yet grounded.

With its rapid pace, rich world-building, and an unpredictable climax, *Enigma Tracer* is a compelling cocktail of brains and brawn. It delivers a perfect mix of action and intellect, leaving readers eager for the next installment. Perfect for fans of suspenseful and tech-savvy thrillers, this book is a must-read.

MURDER ON THE MESA

by Marilyn Wright Dayton

A delightful, witty mystery with charming characters, clever twists, and timeless sleuthing—Murder On The Mesa is brilliantly captivating!

Marilyn Wright Dayton's *Murder On The Mesa* is a delightful debut in *The Hightower Mystery Series*. Combining the charm of cozy mysteries with the cleverness of classic whodunits, this book introduces readers to the spunky and sharp-witted 'Cackle Gang.' Led by Weezie Hightower, a retired private investigator, these four spirited ladies prove that solving crimes is a skill that transcends age.

Set against the backdrop of the Arizona mesas, the novel comes alive with vivid descriptions, a gripping murder case, and an ensemble of suspects that keep readers guessing until the very end. Weezie and her sleuthing partner, retired detective Guy Davis, form a dynamic duo whose chemistry and wit make the story even more engaging. The mystery, involving seven suspects and a tight seven-day investigation, is well-paced and cleverly constructed, leaving just the right amount of clues for readers to piece together.

Dayton excels at crafting relatable, lively characters, with the 'Cackle Gang' standing out as a testament to the power of friendship and determination. The narrative feels familiar yet fresh, with shades of *Murder, She Wrote* and Agatha Christie-like intrigue.

While some might find the resolution slightly predictable or the pacing uneven in parts, the book succeeds in delivering a fun, lighthearted read full of charm. A promising start to a series that showcases age as an advantage, *Murder On The Mesa* offers readers a cozy, satisfying mystery. It's an enjoyable pick for fans of traditional detective tales with a modern twist.

THE SAFEHOUSE

by T. Thomas Ackerman

A thought-provoking and thrilling fantasy that explores the delicate balance between utopia and chaos, offering a captivating start to an epic saga.

T. Thomas Ackerman's *The Safehouse* is a gripping and deeply moving novel that shines a spotlight on the pervasive issue of domestic violence while celebrating the strength, resilience, and solidarity of women. With its compelling narrative, the story teeters between high-stakes drama and heartfelt moments, creating an emotional tapestry that is both heart-wrenching and uplifting.

Detective Jessica Warren is a standout protagonist: fiercely intelligent, empathetic, and determined to make a difference in a world where domestic violence victims often fall through the cracks of the justice system. The novel skillfully portrays Jessie's relentless efforts to protect women who are trapped in abusive situations, weaving together tales of survival and transformation as victims begin to reclaim their lives. The safehouse itself becomes a beacon of hope — a symbol of what can be achieved when people band together to fight for justice and change.

Ackerman doesn't shy away from the harsh realities of domestic abuse, presenting a sobering look at the inadequacies of existing laws while offering a glimpse of what justice could look like. The tension is heightened by the challenges Jessie faces within her own department, particularly the disapproval of a colleague who questions her unconventional methods. This subplot adds depth to the narrative, exploring themes of institutional resistance and personal integrity.

Beyond its enthralling plot, *The Safehouse* carries a meaningful purpose, as 25% of the author's royalties are donated to the National Coalition Against Domestic Violence. This connection underscores the novel's authenticity and heartfelt advocacy for change. A compelling read that is equal parts social commentary and suspense, this book is sure to leave a lasting impact.

THE VEIL OF TIME

by L. M. Montes

A captivating blend of mystery, fantasy, and emotion, 'The Veil of Time' mesmerises with rich characters and gripping twists.

The Veil of Time, the first installment in L. M. Montes' *Time Series*, is an enthralling foray into a world where the past, present, and future intertwine. Both gripping and imaginative, the story pairs elements of mystery, family drama, and an ever-thickening sense of destiny that keeps readers turning the pages.

The protagonist, Tora Jasper, returns to her hometown of East Tawas, Michigan, intending to settle her late parents' affairs and move on. What she discovers among their belongings plunges her into a whirlwind of secrets and revelations, leading her to confront both her family's hidden past and the cosmic forces shaping her future. Montes skillfully balances Tora's personal journey of grief and self-discovery with her awakening to a broader, fantastical quest.

The supporting characters, particularly Kyle Stevens and John Cummings, offer richness to the narrative, each harbouring mysteries that enmesh brilliantly with the plot. Meanwhile, the antagonist, the enigmatic Black Mamba, brings an ever-present shadow of danger that raises the stakes. Montes' portrayal of Tora's tension between light and darkness is riveting, adding emotional conflict to the fast-paced adventure.

The novel's pacing is strong, though certain moments could have benefitted from greater detail to deepen the immersion. Nonetheless, the story is captivating, the stakes are palpable, and the twists invigorate the plot. Michael Montes' illustrative touch adds an atmospheric dimension to the Kindle edition.

For fans of time-travel adventures with a blend of romance and suspense, *The Veil of Time* is a must-read. Montes presents a deeply layered narrative brimming with emotion, discovery, and danger. The cliffhanger ensures that readers will eagerly anticipate the next instalment. A compelling 5-star debut for the series.

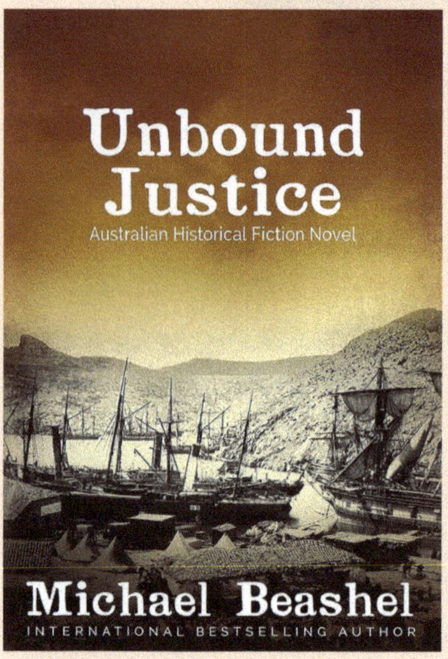

UNBOUND JUSTICE

by Michael Beashel

'Unbound Justice' offers a compelling blend of ambition, love, and revenge in 19th-century Sydney. Rich historical detail and vivid characters make it a captivating start to 'The Australian Sandstone Series'.

Michael Beashel's *Unbound Justice*, the inaugural installment in *The Australian Sandstone Series*, is a richly crafted tapestry of ambition, love, revenge, and resilience set against the backdrop of 19th-century Sydney. This historical fiction novel brims with vivid imagery, robust characters, and gripping drama that plunges readers into the tumultuous era of Australia's gold rush and the burgeoning colony's architectural splendour.

The narrative follows John Leary, an Irishman whose journey to New South Wales is fuelled by more than just dreams of fortune. With a burning desire for justice against William Baxterhouse, the villain who wronged his family, John's story intertwines vengeance with ambition. The contrast between John's steadfast determination to build a construction empire and Baxterhouse's relentless pursuit of power creates a compelling rivalry that builds to a climactic confrontation.

Beashel's portrayal of 19th-century Sydney is both immersive and striking, capturing the contrasting elements of squalor and grandeur, corruption and high-minded aspiration. The city itself becomes a character, its construction serving as a poignant metaphor for growth amidst adversity. The emotional undercurrents are equally gripping, with romantic entanglements—especially between John, Clarissa McGuire, and Beth O'Hare—adding layers of complexity to the tale.

While the novel's pacing occasionally falters with moments of heavy exposition, the strength of its characters and rich historical context more than compensate. *Unbound Justice* is an evocative entrée into a family saga that promises to enchant fans of historical fiction. Whether drawn by its themes of love and retribution or the ambitious spirit of its protagonist, readers will find much to appreciate in this engaging start to the series.

DRAWN FROM LIFE

by Sarah P. Blanchard

A compelling legal drama with political intrigue, featuring a strong, relatable protagonist. Engaging, thought-provoking, and thoroughly captivating.

Sarah P. Blanchard's *Drawn from Life* is an engrossing psychological suspense novel that masterfully dives into the murky waters of guilt, memory, and resilience. This intricately plotted story centres on Emma Gillen, a young woman grappling with the aftermath of a devastating car crash that has robbed her of both her physical health and her memory of the tragedy.

Blanchard expertly weaves layers of tension as Emma faces the return of her manipulative cousin Lucy, whose arrival threatens to unravel long-suppressed truths about Emma's past. Lucy's mercurial nature and insatiable greed are portrayed with chilling precision, making her a compelling and unpredictable foil to Emma's vulnerable yet determined quest for answers.

While the narrative explores dark and complex themes—such as trauma, shame, and betrayal—it also offers a glimmer of hope through Emma's burgeoning inner strength and the quiet support of a compassionate detective. Blanchard's writing is vivid, painting not only the rugged Appalachian setting but also the emotional landscapes of her characters with equal skill. The mounting suspense keeps readers on edge, while the unfolding mystery delves into the fragility and reliability of memory.

Drawn from Life is much more than a suspenseful page-turner; it's an evocative exploration of resilience and the human capacity for redemption in the face of profound hardship. Blanchard's ability to craft complex characters and a high-stakes mystery cements her reputation as a gifted storyteller. Highly recommended for fans of psychological thrillers saturated with emotional depth and raw intensity.

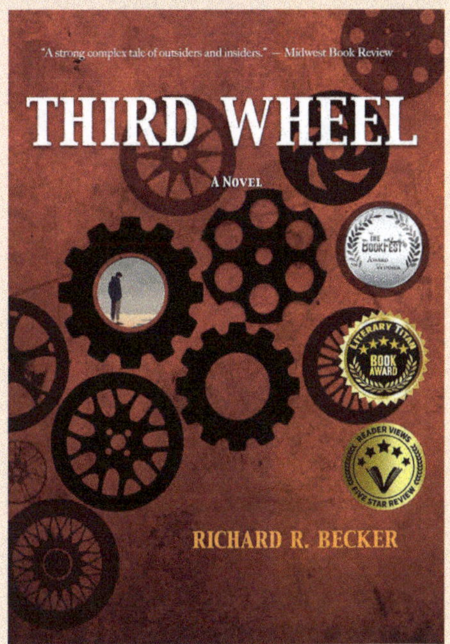

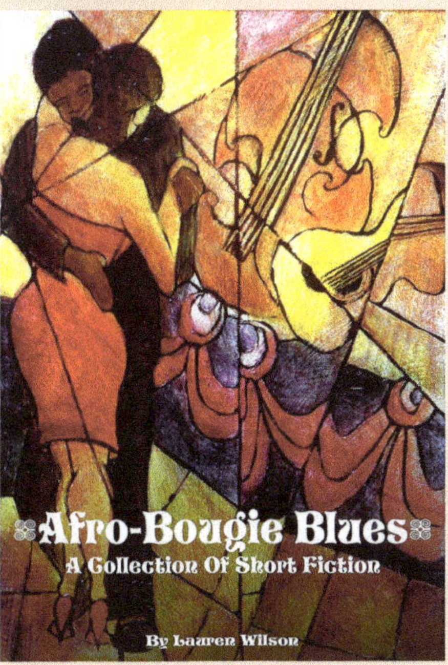

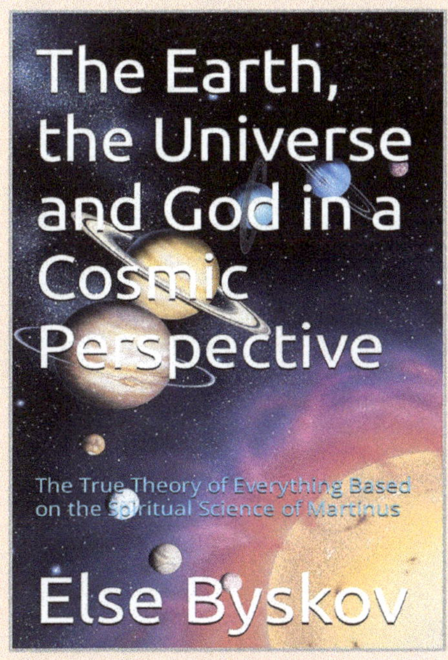

THIRD WHEEL

by Richard R Becker

"Third Wheel' is a captivating, award-winning debut that masterfully blends suspense, emotional depth, and authentic coming-of-age storytelling.

Richard R. Becker's *Third Wheel* is a masterful coming-of-age thriller that expertly balances suspense, emotional depth, and a gritty exploration of adolescence. Set against the backdrop of a desert boomtown in the 1980s, the novel captures the turbulence of teenage life with remarkable authenticity and heart.

The protagonist, Brady Wilks, is a character who will resonate deeply with readers. His struggle to belong, paired with the lure of a dangerous crowd, creates a compelling journey of self-discovery. Becker's nuanced portrayal of Brady's descent into the world of ambition, betrayal, and risky choices keeps the narrative gripping while also painting a poignant picture of vulnerability and resilience.

The strength of *Third Wheel* lies in its multi-layered storytelling. Becker explores themes of belonging, loyalty, and the consequences of impulsive decisions, all while maintaining a sense of urgency that propels the story forward. The relationships between the characters—particularly Brady's complicated ties to Mick and his fragile romance with an older girl—are sharply observed and painfully real, adding emotional weight to the escalating stakes.

Becker's writing is both evocative and unflinching, immersing readers in the suburban shadows of a boomtown swept by change. The pacing is taut and the tension palpable, making it nearly impossible to put the book down.

With six literary accolades to its name, *Third Wheel* is an exceptional debut novel that cements Richard R. Becker as a modern storyteller of rare calibre. A must-read for anyone who appreciates thoughtful, suspenseful fiction with an emotional core.

AFRO-BOUGIE BLUES

by Lauren Wilson

'Afro-Bougie Blues' is a powerful, deeply moving collection of stories, showcasing resilience, authenticity, and the beauty of human strength.

Lauren Wilson's *Afro-Bougie Blues* is an evocative collection of twelve short stories that explore the raw and intimate struggles of ordinary Black women and men navigating life's trials. With heartfelt prose and multifaceted characters, Wilson has crafted a body of work that is both relatable and deeply compelling.

Each story offers a slice of life, delving into thought-provoking themes such as depression, addiction, PTSD, abortion, colourism, and love in its many forms. The narratives are told through different first-person perspectives, drawing the reader into the minds and emotions of characters like Alexis, who faces her past as she discovers love after years of solitude, and Rodney, a war veteran grappling with his demons through alcohol. Stories like Bessie's transformative journey from stagnation to self-discovery and Aisha's childlike yet profound inquiry into love further enrich this anthology. Through every tale, the prose remains poignant, immersing you in the characters' complex worlds.

What stands out most about *Afro-Bougie Blues* is Wilson's ability to blend moments of heartache with glimmers of hope. Her narratives highlight the resilience of the human spirit in the face of adversity, reminding readers of the power of growth and redemption. The stories' emotional depth is enriched by Wilson's vivid storytelling, which challenges readers to reflect on their own assumptions and perspectives.

Whether you are drawn to tales of personal transformation or enjoy exploring diverse human experiences, *Afro-Bougie Blues* is a moving and thought-provoking read. It's a testament to the strength and vulnerability of the everyday person, artfully rendered with authenticity and empathy. A truly remarkable collection.

THE EARTH, THE UNIVERSE AND GOD IN A COSMIC PERSPECTIVE

by Else Byskov

An enlightening masterpiece offering profound insights into life's mysteries, blending spiritual science, cosmic wisdom, and transformative understanding seamlessly.

Else Byskov's *The Earth, the Universe and God in a Cosmic Perspective* offers an awe-inspiring exploration of some of humanity's most profound questions. Drawing upon the spiritual science of Martinus, a Danish visionary whose work is little known outside certain circles, the book seeks to bridge the gap between belief and knowledge, aiming to transform speculative faith into foundational understanding.

Byskov masterfully distils Martinus' vast insights into a concise yet profound narrative, tackling universal curiosities about life's purpose, the nature of God, and the mechanics of the universe. The book positions itself as a guide to achieving "cosmic consciousness," encouraging readers to view their existence from an elevated, holistic perspective. It boldly asserts that Martinus' revelations represent the pinnacle of spiritual insight, offering a luminous path forward for those yearning to comprehend life's greater design.

What sets this work apart is its wide-ranging scope, addressing topics from life after death to creating a peaceful planet. Each concept is handled with a clarity and depth that will appeal to both spiritual seekers and philosophical thinkers. There's a touching optimism woven throughout, championing the idea that humanity can transcend its challenges through heightened awareness and love.

For those unfamiliar with Martinus' spiritual science, the book serves as an accessible yet profound introduction. Its logical organisation and compassionate tone make transformative concepts feel attainable rather than esoteric. While some readers may find the material dense at times, the effort to engage deeply is abundantly rewarded.

Overall, this is a thought-provoking read that has the potential to alter one's worldview entirely. Highly recommended for those ready to explore life's mysteries through a profound spiritual lens.

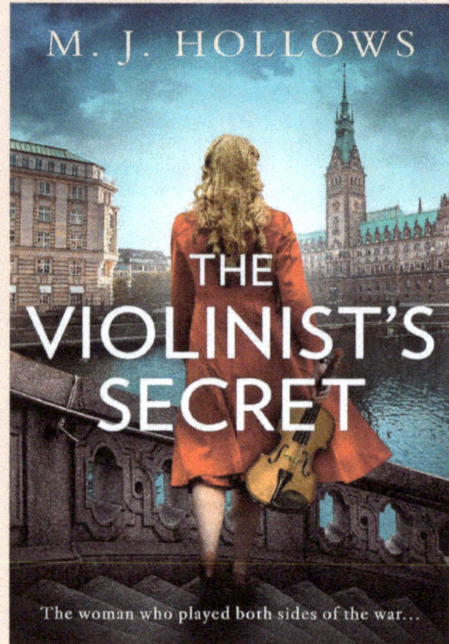

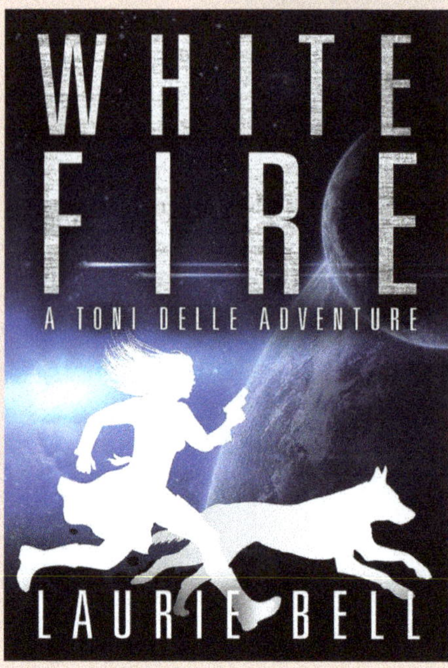

THE VIOLINIST'S SECRET

by M.J. Hollows

Engaging, thought-provoking, and richly detailed, this novel captivates with compelling characters, vivid atmosphere, historical depth, and suspenseful storytelling mastery.

M.J. Hollows delivers an engrossing and suspense-filled tale with *The Violinist's Secret*, a World War II spy novel that deftly blends historical fiction with personal drama. Set in the ominous landscape of Nazi Germany, the story follows Charlotte Weber, a university student whose life takes a sharp turn when she finds herself entangled in both espionage and a dangerous hunt for the truth about her friend Greta's death.

The narrative is rich in atmosphere, capturing the tension and fear in Hamburg under Nazi rule. Hollows pulls readers into Charlotte's inner struggles—whether it's navigating her role as an unwilling spy, grappling with the horrors around her, or keeping her own secrets safe. The violin motif adds a poignant note of resilience and human connection amidst the darkness.

What makes this novel stand out is its exploration of moral ambiguity. Charlotte is not a perfect heroine; she is flawed and thrust into impossible choices, making her journey feel deeply authentic. The plot twists and turns as secrets are revealed, and the suspense keeps you turning the pages.

However, while the storyline is compelling, the pacing occasionally lags, particularly in the middle chapters where the intrigue could have been tighter. Some secondary characters feel underdeveloped, leaving readers wishing for more depth to complement the complex protagonist.

The Violinist's Secret is a gripping and thought-provoking read. Fans of historical fiction and spy thrillers will find much to admire, and Hollows proves once again why she is a master of this genre. A solid 4 out of 5 stars.

WHITE FIRE

by Laurie Bell

Laurie Bell masterfully blends sharp wit, gripping action, and compelling characters in 'White Fire', crafting an unforgettable sci-fi adventure.

Laurie Bell's *White Fire* is a gripping, fast-paced science fiction adventure that will keep readers hooked from start to finish. Starring the fiercely independent yet delightfully flawed Agent Toni Delle, the story falls squarely into the high-stakes, action-packed space opera genre. From shady characters to galaxy-spanning intrigue, the novel thrives on suspense, betrayal, and razor-sharp banter.

Toni Delle is a brilliant protagonist—snarky, resourceful, and stubborn, with just the right amount of vulnerability to make her relatable. Surrounding her are two memorable companions: Mate, her loyal canine robot, and Zach, her sarcastic and witty shipboard intelligence interface. Their interactions bring levity and charm to an otherwise tense and gritty mission. Together, they face a dangerous task: unravelling a deadly smuggling ring tied to an ominous new weapon. Yet, as is often the case with adventures like this, nothing is what it seems, leaving readers on edge as secrets unravel and trust is tested.

Bell's world-building is vivid and immersive, blending advanced technology, intergalactic espionage, and morally ambiguous characters. The narrative's twists and turns make for a gripping read, especially with the enigmatic Smuggler adding layers of mystery and unease to the plot.

With a perfect mix of action, humour, and emotional depth, *White Fire* introduces a heroine and a world readers will want to revisit. Laurie Bell masterfully delivers a space adventure brimming with tension, wit, and heart. Fans of sci-fi thrillers and strong female leads will find this a thrilling new addition to their shelves.

SULTRY, IS THE NIGHT

by Barbara Avon

Barbara Avon's evocative prose, vivid imagery, and emotional depth make 'Sultry, Is the Night' a hauntingly unforgettable read.

Barbara Avon's *Sultry, Is the Night* invites readers on a haunting, atmospheric journey through the complexities of love, loss, and resilience, richly steeped in 1980s nostalgia. Set against the backdrop of a gritty, downtrodden city, the story follows Mario, a son grappling with the demise of his mother. Her passing marks a turning point in Mario's life, inciting both anger and deep vulnerability as he confronts the ghosts of their fractured relationship and his own sense of isolation.

Avon's writing is achingly lyrical, punctuated by vivid descriptions and poignant metaphors that elevate even the darkest moments of the story. From the haze of cigarette smoke against parched brick walls to the grim, discarded remnants of city life, the novel's imagery captures a world brimming with desolation while hinting at Mario's profound inner turmoil. Moreover, Avon doesn't shy away from exploring sensitive themes, delivered with a raw, unapologetic honesty.

What sets this novel apart is its dual nature—it is not only a tale of grief but also a love story. Avon seamlessly weaves in themes of redemption and emotional growth, redirecting the protagonist's journey from despair to self-discovery. That said, *Sultry, Is the Night* is not for the faint-hearted. The strong language and darker themes may unsettle some readers, but they serve to underscore the gravity of the characters' struggles and the rawness of human experience.

For fans of evocative prose and character-driven narratives, this novel is a gripping, melancholic exploration of life's messy edges. Avon's use of 80s-inspired nostalgia adds a poignant layer to a story that ultimately speaks to the healing power of love.

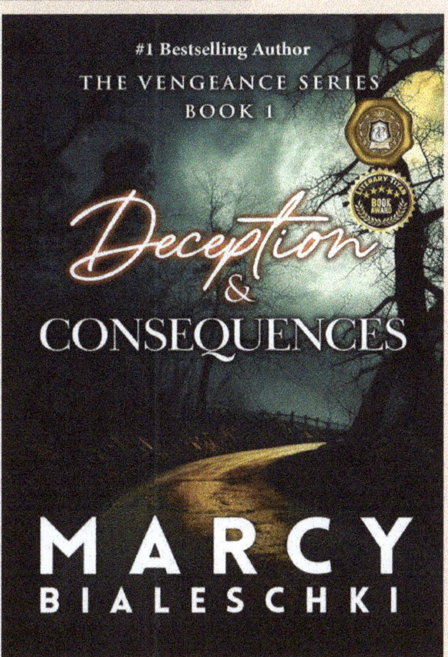

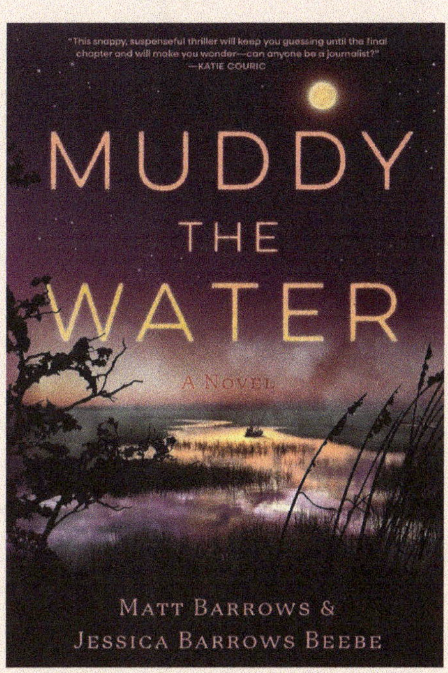

ENIGMA TRACER

by Charles Breakfield and Rox Burkey

An electrifying mix of tech intrigue, action, and suspense; "Enigma Tracer" captivates with compelling characters and an unpredictable plot.

Hope Brooks' memoir, *A Mother's Survival: Finding Balance Through the Storms*, is an inspiring and heartfelt account of resilience, love, and unwavering determination. Written with raw honesty, it takes readers through her extraordinary journey, from a childhood marred by trauma to the struggles and triumphs of building a blended family.

Brooks' story is deeply personal yet universally relatable, offering insights into the myriad challenges life can throw at us — and the strength required to overcome them. She bravely recounts her experiences as a survivor of childhood abuse, the emotional turmoil of supporting a spouse with bipolar disorder, and the daunting task of raising her family after being abandoned. Her ability to rise above these hardships is both humbling and empowering.

The narrative, though often laden with sorrow and strife, is ultimately uplifting. Brooks shares not only the trials of her personal life but also the challenges she faced as a New York City teacher, adding another layer of complexity to her tale. Her message of perseverance resonates throughout the book, inspiring her readers to keep pushing forward, no matter how dire life's circumstances may seem.

While the pacing occasionally feels uneven, the sincerity and warmth of Brooks' voice more than compensate. Her story is a testament to the human spirit and the enduring power of hope.

For those in search of a motivational and deeply moving read, Brooks' memoir will surely leave an indelible mark. It's a compelling reminder that, even in life's darkest storms, balance and strength can be found.

DECEPTION & CONSEQUENCES

by Marcy Bialeschki

A delightful, witty mystery with charming characters, clever twists, and timeless sleuthing—Murder On The Mesa is brilliantly captivating!

Deception & Consequences is an intriguing start to *The Vengeance Series*, blending romance, suspense, and family drama into a gripping narrative. Marcy Bialeschki crafts a story that keeps readers hooked, with its relentless pace and a heroine they can truly root for.

Aria Donaldson, the bold and fiercely independent protagonist, is both relatable and inspiring. Her unexpected encounter with Simon Longoria on a sun-soaked beach in St. Lucia spirals into a tale of danger, passion, and long-hidden family secrets. The novel cleverly intertwines Aria's steamy romance with Mac Brunner—the dependable, swoon-worthy hero—with the darker elements of betrayal and vengeance lurking around every corner.

Bialeschki's ability to create vibrant characters shines throughout the book, particularly in her depiction of Aria's perseverance and Mac's unwavering devotion. The chemistry between them crackles and adds depth to a thriller-paced plot. The antagonist, Deuce Halprin, is suitably sinister, elevating the stakes and keeping the tension palpable.

While *Deception & Consequences* delivers plenty of twists and action, it doesn't shy away from emotional weight either. The themes of family loyalty, generational conflict, and self-discovery give the story layers beyond its surface thrills.

That said, the occasional overly descriptive passages could slow the pace for some readers. But overall, this is a well-crafted and satisfying read that will leave fans eager to follow Aria's journey in the next instalment. Highly recommended for those who enjoy romantic suspense with a gritty edge.

MUDDY THE WATER

Matt Barrows, Jessica Barrows Beebe

Gripping, suspenseful, and masterfully written, 'Muddy the Water' captivates with its complex characters, unpredictable twists, and sharp storytelling. Brilliant!

Muddy the Water is an exceptional debut novel from Matt Barrows and Jessica Barrows Beebe, and it certainly lives up to its accolades. Winning the Literary Global Book Award for Debut Fiction was no fluke—this gripping thriller delivers an enthralling ride from start to finish.

Set against the vivid backdrop of the South Carolina coast, the story plunges into the murky waters of journalism, murder, and identity. The murder of a charismatic fishing captain in Massachusetts sets the stage, but the real intrigue unfolds when Ben Broome—the prime suspect—reinvents himself as a reporter for a struggling southern newspaper. The duality of Ben's character is chilling, as he balances his charm with a dark, sinister cunning that keeps readers on edge.

The narrative's structure, told through the perspectives of the killer, the driven Detective Lillian Grimes, and the ambitious reporter Florence Park, adds impressive depth and complexity. Each character's voice is distinct, and their motivations are expertly woven into the plot. The way the authors explore themes of identity—who we are versus who we present ourselves to be—adds a layer of psychological intrigue.

Barrows and Beebe's prose is sharp and urgent, making for a fast-paced read that brims with suspense. The twists come thick and fast, culminating in a finale that is as satisfying as it is surprising.

Muddy the Water is more than just a thriller; it's a masterfully crafted exploration of morality, ambition, and human nature. A standout debut that will leave readers eagerly anticipating what comes next from this talented duo. Highly recommended!

The Birth of Metaphorical Realism

Vladimir Kush Redefines Surrealism with Metaphorical Realism, Blending Imagination and Nature in a Visionary Artistic Journey

ART & MEDIA

Vladimir Kush is a renowned contemporary artist and the founder of "*Metaphorical Realism,*" a unique artistic style that blends realism with metaphorical imagination. His works, displayed in galleries worldwide and in his own "Kush Fine Art" galleries, invite viewers to explore hidden connections between seemingly unrelated elements, offering a fresh perspective on the world.

Kush describes Metaphorical Realism as the art of discovering hidden likenesses between objects and connecting them in unexpected yet harmonious ways. Unlike traditional surrealism, which often distorts reality, his style emphasizes the internal similarities between realistic objects, creating a romantic and imaginative view of the world. For Kush, the goal is to reflect life through metaphor, finding parallels for every aspect of existence.

Metaphor, for Kush, is more than a linguistic tool—it is a way of understanding and communicating. Through metaphor, he stimulates the subconscious, awakening the viewer's imagination. He likens this process to Plato's concept of the "cave," where human souls retain core ideas of the world. Kush's art serves as a catalyst for this subconscious recollection, allowing viewers to see the familiar in a new light. "Imagination is more important than knowledge," he emphasizes, as imagination creates connections between seemingly unrelated elements.

Kush's journey from a struggling artist to an internationally acclaimed visionary is a story of perseverance. Growing up in Moscow, he was deeply influenced by classical art, literature, and the cultural values of his family. His father, a mathematician and poet, played a pivotal role in shaping his artistic sensibilities. In 1990, Kush made the bold decision to stay in the United States, embarking on a challenging path of self-discovery. From drawing portraits on the beaches of Santa Monica to establishing his own galleries, Kush's journey is a testament to his relentless pursuit of his vision.

The 1990s were a formative period for Kush, marked by relentless effort and the search for his unique style. By 1998, his hard work bore fruit, and he emerged as the founder of Metaphorical Realism. Iconic works like *Wind, Fauna in La Mancha, Bound for Distant Shores, and Music of the Woods* became defining examples of his method, laying the foundation for his artistic legacy.

Kush's creativity extends beyond painting. He has ventured into sculpture, jewelry, and even interactive apps for children, translating his artistic concepts across various mediums. "*Sculptures and jewelry allow me to add another dimension to my ideas,*" he explains. This versatility demonstrates the universality of metaphor, proving that it can exist not only in words and paintings but also in three-dimensional forms.

While Kush cites Salvador Dali as an influence, his artistic journey was shaped by a diverse range of inspirations. His father, despite being a mathematician, was his first teacher, nurturing his love for art from an early age. Kush's artistic evolution began with Renaissance art, transitioned through Impressionism, and eventually found its voice in Surrealism. However, it was the French artist Claude Verlinde who had the greatest impact on his work.

Kush's approach to Surrealism diverges from the darker tones of Dali's era, which were shaped by war and crisis. Instead, Kush introduces a fresh, positive perspective, harmonizing his art with nature and celebrating the beauty of the world. "For the first time in art history, I have introduced a positive side of Surrealism," he says, highlighting the originality of his vision.

Kush's art has been showcased in prestigious galleries and exhibitions worldwide, from South Korea to Russia and the United States. Despite his international acclaim, Kush believes that inspiration comes from within. "If there is inner emptiness, the whole world cannot fill it," he asserts. His art transcends cultural boundaries, inviting viewers from all walks of life to see the world through the mirror of metaphor.

Vladimir Kush's contributions to contemporary art are profound and enduring. As the pioneer of Metaphorical Realism, he has redefined the way we perceive and connect with the world. His art, rich in imagination and cultural depth, serves as a bridge between the material and the metaphorical, the real and the surreal. Through his paintings, sculptures, and other creative endeavors, Kush continues to inspire audiences worldwide, reminding us of the beauty and interconnectedness of life.

Vladimir Kush is a masterful artist whose visionary works redefine surrealism, inspiring awe with their depth, imagination, and beauty.

> *"Imagination is more important than knowledge."*
>
> **Vladimir Kush**

Art as a Bridge Between Personal and Public Narratives

Danica Dakić, a visionary artist whose work has been profoundly shaped by her experiences during the Bosnian War and the siege of Sarajevo, continues to captivate audiences with her exploration of identity, collectivity, and the interplay between personal and public narratives. An interview conducted with the artist for Mosaic Digest delves into the transformative impact of these experiences on her artistic vision and practice.

The war in Bosnia and the subsequent isolation from her homeland marked a pivotal shift in Dakić's artistic journey. During this period, she grappled with the meaning and function of art, leading her to explore new themes, media, and methods. Her installation "Blaues Auge" (1996) exemplifies this shift, addressing the disconnection between personal experience and media narratives. By collaging thousands of newspaper photos and headlines on transparent foil, Dakić created a powerful visual barrier that symbolized the opacity of media representations during times of conflict. This work, and others like it, reflect her ongoing artistic engagement with the tension between personal and public narratives.

Dakić's video installation "Grand Organ" (2010), commissioned for the Touched exhibition at St. George's Hall in Liverpool, further exemplifies her innovative approach to art. Inspired by the hall's majestic organ and neoclassical architecture, the installation explores themes of justice, performance, and music. By transforming the boys' choir into an organ with human pipe voices, composer Bojan Vuletić's sound design highlights the interplay between the legal system and spectacle. The involvement of local choirs, including the Liverpool Signing Choir and the "Sparrows" of Sparrow Hall, underscores Dakić's focus on polyphony and childhood, creating a narrative that examines power dynamics and community.

Throughout her career, Dakić has experimented with various mediums, from painting to video, sound, and text. Her choice of medium is driven by the narrative or message she wishes to convey, with each medium offering a unique way to experience her images. As an "image maker," Dakić believes in the power of images to communicate complex ideas and emotions that transcend traditional media boundaries.

Dakić's work is deeply informed by historical and social contexts, particularly in relation to identity and collectivity. While her personal experiences of war and displacement influence her exploration of these themes, her art speaks to universal experiences of mobility, migration, and living in multiple languages and cultures. Her work invites viewers to reflect on the perception of the global present and the role of the individual within larger societal structures.

The tension between individuality and collectivity is a recurring theme in Dakić's art, as seen in the allegorical references to music and law in "Grand Organ." She explores this tension on visual, acoustic, performative, and emotional levels, offering a nuanced perspective on the individual's place within society. Her art challenges viewers to consider the complexities of identity and the interconnectedness of personal and collective experiences.

Danica Dakić's artistic journey is a testament to her resilience and creativity in the face of adversity. Her work continues to inspire and provoke thought, offering a powerful commentary on the human condition and the ever-evolving narratives that shape our world. Through her innovative use of media and exploration of profound themes, Dakić has established herself as a leading voice in contemporary art, captivating audiences with her ability to transform personal experiences into universal narratives.

Dakić's experiences during the Bosnian War reshaped her artistic vision, leading to new themes and media explorations.

ART & MEDIA

Danica Dakić is a visionary artist whose profound insights and creativity transform personal experiences into universal narratives.

"The war had a strong influence on my life and my art."

Capturing the Pulse of the Modern City

Brendan Neiland reflects on his artistic evolution, from peaceful landscapes to bustling cities, and shares how urban reflections, vibrant colors, and dynamic architecture became the heart of his creative expression.

BRENDAN NEILAND

THE POWER OF MODERN METROPOLITAN LIFE AS A MUSE

as told to Archie Preston

“Brendan Neiland in his studio, where his passion for urban reflections and architectural forms takes shape on canvas.”

Brendan Neiland's work captures the essence of urban life in a way few others can, transforming everyday cityscapes into vibrant, reflective wonders. Known for his fascination with architectural forms, mirrored surfaces, and the dynamic, pulsating energy of metropolitan settings, Neiland invites viewers to see cities as multi-layered compositions of light, colour, and structure. His art draws you in, reflecting the compelling contrast of grand scale and intricate detail, capturing the dichotomy of intimacy within enormity that defines city life. Through decades of dedication, his works have become iconic portrayals of the modern urban experience, reflecting his unique ability to blend meticulous technical skill with an emotional depth that resonates universally.

Neiland shares insights into his creative journey—from his formative years in East Anglia and Birmingham to his lifelong captivation with cities around the globe. His story unveils how the stark transition from pastoral landscapes to urban vitality shaped his artistic vision, instilling a fascination with the scale, dynamism, and vibrancy of urban environments. Neiland's commitment to capturing the energy of city life, often through countless hours spent observing, walking, and photographing, becomes the foundation of his art—a dedication to portraying the allure

ART & MEDIA

Brendan Neiland's vibrant abstract composition invites viewers into a dynamic exploration of urban life, where bold colors and geometric patterns reflect the pulsating energy of cityscapes. Each section of the painting captures the intricate interplay of light and structure, embodying Neiland's fascination with the modern metropolis and his journey from the serene landscapes of East Anglia to the vibrant streets of Birmingham and beyond.

of modernity in all its raw and polished forms.

How has your background and education influenced your approach to painting and printmaking?

I lived in East Anglia until I was fourteen, peaceful, blissful, huge skies with lush flat meadows. And then I moved to Birmingham.

> Brendan Neiland's mastery lies in his ability to capture the beauty, complexity, and vibrancy of urban life with profound emotional resonance.

Amazing, all embracing. From Constable to Fernand Leger.

This altered my life,I felt exhilarated. it was so exciting to live in a place so vibrant...

Everything, the size, activity, noise, the shops and factories, it was so vital and I loved it.

I attended St. Phillip's a Catholic school run by the Oratorians. I went from there to the White Fathers seminary in the depths of Ireland. Here I spent a highly organised and disciplined two years studying philosophy and preparing for the priesthood. The Father Superior encouraged me in my art, painting and creating. Through dyed sawdust, I created huge heads of saints which were destroyed by the processions on feast days.

I did however miss the world and left Ireland to join Birmingham Art School Strangely the change was not anywhere as extreme as I had anticipated,

to be a priest or an artist both demand complete dedication and commitment.

I spent some months in various factories making colour studies of the huge iron ingots being smelted and turned into beautiful parts for ships and cars.

In 1996 I was accepted inti the painting school of the RCA. An extraordinary and very formative environment, led by Carel Weight with Peter Blake, Dick Smith and Jim Dine.

Your art often reflects themes of modern metropolitan existence. What aspects of urban life do you find most inspiring or challenging?

The City became my subject matter. Starting with machine parts, then cars, the environment reflected in the car bodies and finally the buildings of the city.

Since Birmingham I have lived in and visited cities worldwide

My first visit to New York City in the early seventies shocked and stunned me. It was exhilarating. I have made a pilgrimage every year since.

Exhibitions and commissions and desire have taken me, amongst others, to Singapore, Hong Kong, Shanghai, Central America and many cities within Europe The strangest experience being Las Vegas, pure theatre, no night or day pure enticement.

I walk and walk looking listening and soaking up the atmosphere.

I always have a camera. The photographs provide a reminder and a visual support in the studio but it is the walking and being totally immersed in the environment that is primarily important.

At first the city buildings provided my inspiration with the reflections of the sky and the traffic. Gradually the advertisements with their powerful colour, the displays in the shop windows, the extraordinary crowds within the city centres the multitude of languages feed into the paintings. City centres are incredibly enticing, the displays and the advertisements are huge catalysts and ever present in our daily lives

How do you balance the intimate and grand elements in your artwork, and what do you hope viewers take away from this contrast?

I want the excitement and awe that I feel to be present in my paintings

The architecture and all of the other elements that make up the city strive for a certain perfection through form material and colour to win over the approbation of us all

A way of life is being displayed, one that is so rich and desirable

I immerse myself in it. I Love it and it provides my inspiration

Crafting Dreams and Dualities in Modern Art

Artist Brian Hubble blends fine detail with surreal, expressive imagery, using image-transfer techniques to create pieces that explore the relationship between images, performance, and the unexpected. His work invites contemplation through poetic contrasts.

BRIAN HUBBLE

A DIALOGUE THROUGH DRAWING USING A RANGE OF MATERIALS

By Sam Tylor

"I believe contradictions play a crucial role in dreams—an idea I keep in mind when merging original and classical imagery."

Brian Hubble's artistic journey reads as a tapestry woven from his explorations across continents, styles, and mediums. Rooted in the diverse energy of Brooklyn, New York, for over two decades, Hubble's work carries a deeply reflective quality, channeling experiences from his stints in Italy and Chicago. His art has graced respected spaces like the Museum of Contemporary Art in Chicago and MoMA PS1, while his unique interpretations have been highlighted in the New York Times, Taschen Books, and Print Magazine. Hubble's artistry invites viewers into his meditative creative space, where images blend and transform, balancing meticulous detail with bold, surreal contrast.

An artist with a dedication to defying convention, Hubble's work radiates both intimacy and complexity. He navigates striking contrasts—fine detail meets cartoon simplicity, historical iconography mingles with the everyday, and his pieces explore the relationship between images, performance, and dialogue through drawing, balanced by innovation. Hubble's distinctive image-transfer techniques and reverence for process elevate each piece, cultivating a "dreamy uneasiness" that lingers in the viewer's mind. Here, in this exclusive interview, Hubble shares insights into his world of contradictions, process, and performance—revealing an artist as thoughtful as his creations are unforgettable.

Can you describe how your early experiences with drawing have shaped your current artistic practice?

My earliest memory is of my mother patiently teaching me to draw a spider web when I was five. That experience sparked my curiosity and inspired me to try drawing something more complex, like our family pets or a face. Once I explored those subjects, I felt the need to return to something more immediate, which often

Brian Hubble at work in his Brooklyn studio, crafting layered, evocative pieces that merge detail, surreal elements, and a sense of exploration into art that invites discovery.

manifested as hasty scribbles or crayon markings. These impulsive drawings held as much significance for me as the "harder" pieces. Years later, as an art student, this ebb and flow became a driving force in my work. I was always interested in creating artworks that serve as a rebuttal to those that came before, both in timing and content. I still work this way today.

You mention the use of image transfers in your work. How has this technique evolved over time, and what does it add to your creative process?

As a longtime admirer of Robert Rauschenberg's work, I have always been fascinated by the various techniques for creating image transfers. My version is quick and inexpensive. I print on silicone coated release paper—typically discarded after peeling off envelope labels or stickers. Its surface has just enough coating to retain the printed image yet pliable enough for an effective transfer onto clean paper. I photograph the most successful transfers and refine them as single images in post-production software before integrating them into an overall composition. This method is repeated for every element of a piece until it is nearly exhausted into completion. At this point, an ultraviolet print of the composition is made onto a large sheet of canvas. I work on top of the print with graphite, colored pencils, oil, and pastels. I intentionally leave select areas in their UV print form, exposing colorful yet disquieting backgrounds. This multi-step process allows me to slowly manipulate volume and stillness within the piece.

Hubble's art captivates with its emotional depth and technical mastery, weaving past and present into visionary pieces that redefine artistic boundaries.

Your drawings exhibit a blend of laborious detailing and cartoon flatness. How do you navigate this balance, and what do you hope to convey through these contrasts?

Deciding whether to make a detailed drawing or something quicker depends on the subject at hand, and how previous pieces were created. My next concern is the interaction between each drawing and the surrounding images. I'm constantly tweaking because, for me, one of the joys of being an artist is form discovery. I hope that the forms in my work poetically mingle with tension. I want to share the weary yet hopeful, meditative space I fall into while creating them.

You discuss creating a sense of "dreamy uneasiness" in your work. What specific techniques do you employ to achieve this effect?

I believe contradictions play a crucial role in dreams—an idea I keep in mind when merging original and classical imagery. I collage appropriated art historical figures such as cherubs and charmers, with curious animals and saturated flowers. I assign both familiar and surprising surfaces to the images I draw and paint. For instance, multiple layers of colored pencils can render skin with the translucent quality of marble. Graphite lends drawings of filing cabinets the chill of cold metal, while a combination of materials imparts a warm patina to wood. Illogical yet nuanced scenes feature recurring elements like orbs, rainbows, and patterned landscapes, which blur the line between representation and abstraction.

Your exhibition on Andy Kaufman explores the intersection of art and performance. How do you see your own work reflecting or challenging traditional notions of performance art?

We may someday need to have a separate interview about my time with Andy Kaufman and the exhibition I organized at the Museum of the Moving Image! I spent 16 years studying everything in Andy's world and cherish the friendship I developed with his family during that time in my life. While I experimented with performance art in graduate school, I have since transitioned to a hermetic studio practice. Although I wouldn't say there's a direct line from performance art to the paintings and drawings I'm making now, I like to think that a bit of Andy's spirit is woven into them from time to time.

What role do you believe nostalgia plays in your art, particularly when you incorporate drawings from 20 years ago with your current work?

Incorporating work I made in the past with newer pieces has led to unexpected breakthroughs. When reviewing my previous works, I don't feel a sense of the past or longing for what once was. At the time of making them, I probably didn't fully grasp how they might function down the road. I may have felt they were complete, but perhaps I was mistaken—I'm not entirely sure. I'm interested in introducing them to recent images to hopefully produce something surprising and genuine as a result. Many of these experiments fail, of course, but I suppose the idea is to fail a bit less with each attempt.

Crafting Dreams and Dualities in Modern Art

Artist Brian Hubble blends fine detail with surreal, expressive imagery, using image-transfer techniques to create pieces that explore the relationship between images, performance, and the unexpected. His work invites contemplation through poetic contrasts.

DANIEL CERREJON

A DIALOGUE THROUGH DRAWING USING A RANGE OF MATERIALS

“

The knots are made by tying one after another in a compulsive manner until the rope can no longer be folded.”

ART & MEDIA

Editor's Desk

Daniel Cerrejon is a visionary artist whose work challenges the boundaries between the tangible and the abstract, the personal and the universal. With a career that spans continents and artistic disciplines, Cerrejon has cultivated a practice that is as intellectually rigorous as it is emotionally resonant. His art delves into the intersections of data, objects, and the human body, transforming cold, statistical abstractions into visceral, poetic forms. From his CORPUS series, which reimagines bodily measurements as intricate knots imbued with warmth and humanity, to his exploration of proxemics and relational distances, Cerrejon's work invites viewers to reconsider the ways in which we perceive ourselves and the spaces we inhabit. His ability to balance the technical with the corporeal, the conceptual with the sensory, marks him as a singular voice in contemporary art.

In this interview, Cerrejon offers a rare glimpse into his creative process and the philosophies that underpin his practice. From his early studies in Madrid and New York to his time at the Whitney Independent Study Program, he reflects on the cultural and intellectual influences that have shaped his journey. Through his thoughtful responses, Cerrejon unpacks the layers of meaning in his work, revealing how he transforms data into art and abstraction into intimacy. This conversation is a testament to his profound ability to bridge the gap between the empirical and the emotional, creating art that not only engages the mind but also resonates deeply with the soul.

In the CORPUS series, what significance do the knots and

An abstract representation of connection and preservation, featuring an organic form encased in transparent plastic, symbolizing the delicate balance of human interaction and containment.

flesh-like tones hold in relation to the "cold" statistical language used in the titles?

Each piece in the CORPUS series consists of various components. To answer your question, we can focus on four: the knots, color, titles, and bodily measurements. I appreciate how you frame your question in terms of 'coldness.' To me, two of these components are 'cold'—the measurements and color—while the other two, the knots and titles, feel 'warm.' By 'cold,' I mean purely conceptual elements lacking traditional artistry. The measurements represent body data, while the color comes from covering the knots with makeup in a shade that approximates the average skin tone of the American population at the time the works were made. Each piece in the CORPUS series reflects 'the average American person,' as indicated by the titles.

Daniel Cerrejon masterfully bridges the technical and the emotional, creating art that transforms data into deeply human experiences.

The two elements I consider 'warm,' as opposed to the 'cold' ones, are the knots and titles. Each title in this series combines various standard bodily measurements, arranged in a poetic way. The rules for these poetic titles vary for each piece. Sometimes, the poetry lies in the sound and rhythm of the words, while other times, it emerges from the sequential meaning of specific measurements. An example title from this series is From One Hand to the Other, whilst Each Holds the Other, of the Average American Person.

The last of the four elements we're discussing is the knot, which I described as a 'warm' element in this temperature analogy. Each knot is made by cutting a rope to the length specified in the title and tying it into a continuous knot without a beginning or end. The process of knotting is arbitrary and emotional, created by tying one knot after another in a compulsive manner until the rope can no longer be folded.

Your work brings a visceral, almost tangible presence to abstract measurements. How do you balance the contrast between the technical and the corporeal in your art?

My artwork is the embodiment of data, often related to our bodies, into physical objects. This process involves a back-and-forth between a scientific approach—an empirical method of acquiring knowledge—and an artistic approach, which is more intuitive in solving and understanding a situation. As we discussed, some works begin with a system of bodily measurements. These measurements transform into language, which is articulated in a specific way, and this language, in turn, influences the form of the work. This form is then received by the viewer, shifting their perception of themselves. It is in this final stage, when the work is perceived, that I would describe the experience as visceral. Not only because some pieces resemble guts or internal organs, evoking raw, physical sensations, but also because the perception of objects appeals to physical sensations rather than logical reasoning. I believe this sensory engagement shapes how we understand ourselves. It's not just in artworks; all the objects around us play a role in shaping our self-perception.

Could you share more about your exploration of proxemics in your work? How do you approach representing human relational distances through sculpture?

Proxemics is the study of how people use space and distance in communication, and how these distances can convey meanings, emotions, and social dynamics. In my work, I explore these 'empty distances'—the spaces between people interacting—and transform them into objects. The resulting objects serve as index of an absence.

How does the concept of "average" influence your art, particularly in terms of bodily metrics and flesh tones, and what commentary are you hoping to make on standardization?

I became interested in the concept of the average because it transforms something universal into something particular. The data tables I use in my work are already the result of averaging—data taken from a large group of people within a specific segment of the population, with the average presented as a universal. In my work, I often reverse this process, calculating the average of various universal data points to produce a singular value, which then becomes an art object. The average calculation explores the relationship between the universal and the particular, or the collective and the individual.

By using this averaging method, I break the typical logic of data extraction. While averaging is normally part of data analysis, in my work it serves no practical purpose other than to create art.

For viewers of your work, what emotions or reactions do you hope to evoke as they encounter the embodied and recontextualized measurements in your sculptures?

As I mentioned before, more than emotions or reactions, I'm interested in art and the act of making because of how our surroundings influence our perception of ourselves .Making art is a way for me to engage with the constellation of things around us.

Exploring Passion And Creative Resilience

Gary Petersen explores his journey from Gary Petersen transforms geometric abstraction into vibrant expressions forged from his humble Staten Island origins and refined via transformative residencies and award recognition, bridging contemporary exploration with timeless artistic inquiry.

GARY PETERSEN

ILLUMINATES CONTEMPORARY ABSTRACTION WITH VIBRANT EXPRESSION

Editor's Desk

> "Staten Island is one of the five boroughs that make up New York City, and I grew up there in a lower-middle-class household. My parents did not have a college education, and I attended Catholic schools without any art classes."

ART & MEDIA

Gary Petersen's art is a vivid testament to the power of abstraction—a journey marked by bold color, dynamic shapes, and an inherent sense of rhythm. His work thrusts geometric abstraction into a realm that is both playful and deeply meaningful. With an unmistakable visual language defined by daring compositions and lively, vibrant palettes, Petersen creates paintings that extend beyond the limitations of the canvas; they invite viewers to explore layers of meaning and emotional resonance. Every piece seems to pulse with life, a delicate equilibrium between precision and spontaneity—a balance that speaks to his mastery of form and hue.

Born and raised in Staten Island, one of New York City's five boroughs, Petersen's early environment was a world far removed from the academic art scene. Growing up in a lower-middle-class household and attending Catholic schools without art classes, he was first introduced to the world of art alongside a burgeoning interest in biology. As a first-generation college student, he initially gravitated toward a practical field, choosing to major in Animal Science at Pennsylvania State University with dreams of becoming a

"Gary Petersen's vibrant abstractions balance precision with spontaneity, inviting viewers into a dynamic world of color, movement, and form."

veterinarian. However, a chance elective art class in his junior year revealed his true passion. Socializing among graduate art students, Petersen discovered a creative universe that called him to seize the brush and begin painting.

Gary Petersen is a visionary artistic powerhouse whose fearless innovation, vibrant palette, and masterful abstraction continue to inspire and captivate.

Over the years, transformative residencies have played a crucial role in his creative evolution. Experiences at places like MacDowell and Italy's Bogliasco Foundation have provided him with the rare gift of unhurried exploration—a vital break from everyday distractions. In the sun-drenched Ligurian light of Bogliasco, the interplay of vibrant cityscape hues pushed him to experiment boldly with color. Such residencies not only broaden his creative horizons but also allow him to meet diverse artists, further fueling his artistic vision.

Recognition in the art world has also bolstered his creative journey. The surprise and honor of being awarded The Barnett and Annalee Newman Foundation Grant in 2020 was a turning point. Besides the financial freedom to focus exclusively on his studio work, the grant's legacy lives on as one of Petersen's paintings was acquired for the Newman Foundation collection at New York's Jewish Museum—an accolade that placed him alongside many celebrated artists.

From solo to group exhibitions across New York, Munich, and beyond, Petersen approaches each show with thoughtful intent. In solo exhibitions, he meticulously choreographs the interplay between his work and the chosen space, collaborating closely with gallery professionals to ensure that each stroke and hue engages in an evocative dialogue with its environment. While group shows involve a more passive installation process governed by curators, his vigilant studio practice continues to refine and define his unmistakable signature.

Ultimately, Petersen hopes his work captures not only the gaze but the heart of each viewer—inviting introspection and joy, and offering a narrative that speaks to the immediacy of our present while remaining timeless.

Chenxi Shao's art merges organic materials like mycelium with industrial objects, exploring themes of identity, alienation, and sustainability while addressing ecological and cultural tensions in a post-modern, capitalist world.

Chenxi Shao Explores Identity, Ecology, And Art Through Organic And Industrial Materials

Blending Nature And Culture To Challenge Boundaries

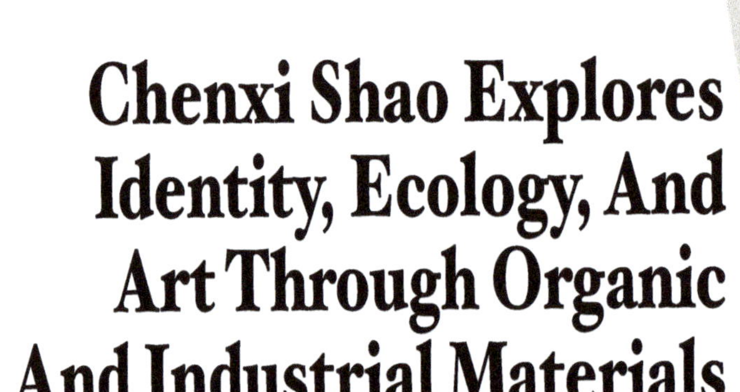

Chenxi Shao is a visionary artist whose work transcends boundaries—geographical, cultural, and material. Born in Tianjin, China, and now based between Beijing and Philadelphia, Chenxi's art is a profound exploration of identity, memory, and ecological ethics. Their practice, which spans sculpture and animation, is deeply informed by their background as an ecological researcher, offering a unique lens through which they examine the intersections of nature, culture, and human experience. With a remarkable ability to weave together the personal and the universal, Chenxi's work challenges conventional narratives and invites us to reconsider our relationship with the world around us.

Chenxi Shao's groundbreaking art redefines materiality, blending innovation and emotion to create profound reflections on identity and ecological ethics.

Chenxi's art is a testament to their innovative spirit and intellectual depth. Their use of organic materials like mycelium and rocks, combined with industrial and everyday objects, creates hybrid forms that are as thought-provoking as they are visually striking. These works not only address pressing environmental concerns but also delve into themes of alienation, identity, and the tension between tradition and modernity. Exhibited in prestigious venues across the globe, Chenxi's creations resonate with a poetic urgency, offering an elegy for life in the face of ecological and societal decay. It is an honor to feature Chenxi Shao in this issue of Magazine, where they share insights into their creative process, inspirations, and the profound messages embedded in their art.

What inspired you to incorporate mycelium and rocks into your art practice?

I began incorporating mycelium into my sculptures after reflecting on personal experiences with cancer and vitiligo in my family. The invasive spread of cancer and the white patches of vitiligo in the body felt like a process of alienation, both physically and emotionally. Mycelium, as it spreads and forms structures with its hyphae, seemed to mimic the biological process of these diseases.

I was also inspired by the book Mushroom: At the End of the World. The idea of mycelium creating a "third nature" within a capitalist framework intrigued me, so I began to explore how it could be used in sculpture.

Rocks, on the other hand, tie back to my interest in the history of the silicon industry. I'm fascinated by how raw materials, like sand, can symbolize a technical gap and an unfinished, evolving process.

Can you share more about the process of growing mushrooms in unusual materials for your artwork?

Initially, I grew mycelium using a ready-made mycelium substance. Inspired by its spreading and growth, I wondered if it could interact with everyday waste materials. So, I started experimenting by combining mycelium with materials like cotton fabric, receipt paper, brown paper, wound paste, disposable masks, and earplugs. For each material, I divided them into three layers and placed them at different levels within the mycelium. After two weeks, the mycelium had grown through all the materials, merging with them in interesting ways.

One of the pieces I created using this process is called Professor, where I grew mycelium with a disposable mask in a mold to form an organic structure. This new material felt exciting and full of potential.

How do you see the relationship between nature and art in your creations?

Nature and art in my work are deeply intertwined. Nature, through mycelium and other organic materials, offers an unexpected form of agency and life that contrasts with the artificial and constructed nature of human-made art. I try to explore how these materials mimic or represent the complexities of identity, alienation, and environmental concerns.

What challenges have you faced while working with organic materials like mycelium?

The biggest challenge has been maintaining an aseptic condition. Mycelium cultivation requires sterilizing the environment to avoid contamination, which is difficult without a proper lab. During my MFA, I had access to a biodesign lab, but since I don't have that access now, I'm exploring alternatives, like using UV light and alcohol to sterilize mycelium in a small room. Achieving a controlled, clean environment is crucial for successful cultivation.

How do you think your work contributes to conversations about sustainability or environmental awareness?

By using bio-materials, my work directly contributes to sustainability by reducing CO2 emissions compared to traditional sculptural materials and processes. However, I also aim to connect environmental concepts with broader social and cultural narratives. My art practice seeks to find new ways of integrating environmental consciousness into art-making, encouraging a dialogue on the potential for more sustainable practices in contemporary art.

Are there specific themes or messages you aim to convey through your art involving natural elements?

The themes of alienation and identity are central to my work. Through living materials like mycelium, I explore how the body grows and changes, but also how it can become alienated. Drawing from the book The Mushroom at the End of the World by Anna Tsing, I use mycelium's function as a decomposer and ecological network to symbolize the spread of disease, bodily decay, and alienation. The hybrid forms I create from industrial materials and natural elements reflect the tension between modern industrial society and the organic world. It's an elegy for life in the midst of capitalist post-modernity and environmental decay.

Terence Hannum discusses The interplay of life, decay technology

A Journey Through Nature's Shadows

***Terence Hannum** explores psychoactive plants in his sculptures, discussing mortality, technology the uncanny, blending art and nature into immersive experiences.*

Renowned for his evocative exploration of the intersection between nature and existence, Terence Hannum's artistic practice seamlessly blends the realms of sculpture, painting technology. With an innovative approach that employs 3D modelling and printing, Hannum's work vividly captures the essence of psychoactive and poisonous plants, inviting viewers to ponder themes of mortality, transformation the uncanny. His installations are not merely static displays but living entities that infiltrate and interact with their surroundings, creating immersive environments that challenge our perceptions of life and decay.

Hannum delves into the inspirations behind his thought-provoking sculptures and the creative processes that inform his unique installations. He reflects on how science fiction influences his artistic vision and the ways in which he manipulates materials and lighting to evoke an otherworldly quality in his work. Join us as we explore the mind of an artist who is reshaping our understanding of botanical forms and their implications for existence, inviting us to confront the delicate balance between beauty and decay.

What drew you to explore the themes of psychoactive and poisonous plants in your sculptures how do they relate to concepts of existence and mortality?

I was drawn to psychoactive and poisonous plants in sculpture mainly through my paintings, I had been painting these plants and then was teaching 3D modelling and decided to try and generate some sculptures with the technology. I thought it could be a good way to have say, a base of forms, leaves, stems, buds, flowers - that could grow as the installation grew. The work relates to existence and mortality in a few ways, one coming out of a still life tradition in the paintings always points to this frozen moment in time, often works would incorporate flowers that do not bloom at the same time, or bugs and elements of decay. However, the sculptures to me kind of grow take over spaces infiltrating the architecture. In a way it is more a comment on our existence, fleeting, overtaken by plants and decay.

Can you describe your creative process when modelling your pieces in 3D software? How does this technology influence the final outcome of your work?

I tend to break down whatever I am trying to model, sometimes it is a very specific flower - jimsonweed or foxglove - or I am mutating or allowing the process to reign over botanical accuracy. My process tends to break down the form, sculpting a petal or flower, then sculpting a leaf or stem and then combing them into different configurations. I tend to start small and combine multiple sculpts into one. It really is beholden to the technology, mainly the 3D printing process, sometimes I don't know until it is complete if it works. I may need to tweak it or the supports are too robust.

In what ways do science fiction and botany intersect in your artistic practice how do they inform the design and presentation of your installations?

I am a huge fan of science fiction, to me it is the uncanny that the genre can allow us to talk about one thing while addressing another. Be it Jeff VanderMeer's "Annihilation" or classics like "Invasion of the Body Snatchers" or "Day of the Triffids" I think it allows us to read it as is, but have beneath it like a larger discussion. For me it is a way of maybe addressing climate change, for example plants that are translucent, not needing sunlight to photosynthesize, these exist in nature anyway, but like what about changing botanical characteristics to make plants parasitic and hostile to our existence.

The installation features translucent flowers with delicate lighting—how do you choose the materials and lighting to enhance the "alien qualities" of your work?

This is really the experiment, I make a lot of small prototypes to see how the material will work and then try different lighting. The shadows kind of make the work. Having them come out of white walls and be translucent or iridescent or glow n the dark kind of gives them this otherworldly quality that I find important. So I experiment a lot with filament or resins and how they appear.

How does your homage to Invasion of the Body Snatchers inform the conceptual and visual elements of your installations, particularly in relation to themes of transformation and reality?

I always found the ideas in Jack Finney's book interesting but probably best expressed in the Kaufman film from 1978. I always loved that every piece of plant life became suspect. And how so many things in the background helped reinforce the idea of this invasion of corrupted doubles. So to me it was more, what is the real one, the one who transformed or the original host who is discarded. I also liked the invented pods and plant life in the film.

With your diverse exhibition history, how do you adapt your work for different gallery spaces what impact do you hope your installations have on the audience?

I tend to think of each exhibition as unique, so the architecture of the space both inside and out are fair game for the installation. If I am proposing something I may focus on a specific unique architectural attribute, like work hanging from the ceiling or continuing outside. For me, the impact I would hope is one of the uncanny, organic sculptural forms overtaking architecture, glowing or feeling like they assist in the decay of the building. That is what I am going for.

Andrés Janacua

Andrés Janacua *delves into the textures of 16mm film, the philosophical nature of moving images, empathy through animals the collaborative spirit that defines his unique approach to contemporary art.*

Andrés Janacua is a voice of profound introspection and subtle provocation in contemporary art, merging heritage with a unique, tactile approach to moving images. Known for his mastery of 16mm film, Janacua's work exudes a layered depth, exploring memory, perception the elusive nature of visual narratives. His pieces engage the viewer with a haze of grain and warmth, fostering a space where images aren't just seen but felt—hovering between familiarity and ambiguity. His work serves as an invitation to question the nature of knowledge, to embrace the unpredictability of perception to find meaning in the unresolved.

This exclusive interview offers readers a glimpse into Janacua's creative world. We discuss his inspirations, from the allure of analog film's physicality to the complexity of working with found images and animal representations. Janacua's reflections on collaboration through Galería Perdida, his evolving artistic philosophy the impact of his varied residency experiences reveal the rich textures and contradictions that animate his practice. As a teacher and artist, Janacua is a true innovator, transforming his multifaceted background into a captivating, boundary-defying art form.

16mm Film as a Medium of Texture and Memory

There's too much liquidity in digital formats... 16mm's limits force contending with what you've captured, for better or worse."

What inspired you to focus on 16mm film and the exploration of moving images in your artistic practice?

I understood that the use of 16mm as a means to create distance, that is, there's enough grain, flare gossamer of colour to push the images back further from the viewer. Oftentimes, this haziness, this atmospheric perspective, lets the images float and linger in the presence of the viewer. I took to the medium for its tactility, warmth familiarity.

I appreciate how moving images are testimonial in nature and I aim to suggest that the presumption of knowledge is to be questioned, or second guessed. It's an epistemological bent that points to gullibility, the nature of taxonomies the slipperiness of images. I am keen to have the moving images result in far more questions than a crisp narrative arc. The frames of film are paths to unravel what things we know and what things we presumed to know.

Can you describe your approach to combining original footage with appropriated materials from the 16mm archive and lantern slide collection?

The majority of the time I shoot original footage that may be culled from images I've seen or collected. Scenes that we reworked and reimagined for the context of the film. From time to time I will combine footage with found footage for its elasticity. I appreciate the tonal quality of this footage and in particular the found images from various sources, including a lantern slide collection courtesy the Visual Studies Workshop in Rochester, NY where I spent a brief moment as an artist in residence. Certain images are prosaic to counter the rest of the images as some can be spectacular. All of these images have an inherent currency. It is this agency that draws me to images that I had no hand in crafting.

Why are you particularly interested in the representation of quadrupeds in your work what do you hope to convey through this focus?

(great question) The desire to use animals, quadrupeds in particular, holds packages of empathy that can be a connective tissue for any given viewer. These creatures, burdensome as they are charming, reflect perhaps the specificity of memory or referent. They are conduits for expressive means of concerns pointing often to bits of humor, frailty, stubbornness, malaise confusion—all naturally human tendencies.

In all honesty, my direct relationship to animals has been at an arm's distance. Growing up in rural Mexico and Los Angeles, these beings were functional things, not repositories of love and care. In this manner they've manifested differently in my response and approach to them. In a way, they too have been anomalous to me, figuring out a way to relate to something I've long neglected.

How has your experience at previous artist residencies, such as at MFAH CORE and Queens Museum, influenced your artistic development and current project?

My privilege of having attended several residencies has afforded me not only the resources of such programs but the fundamental benefit of the time allowed to focus on questions driving my practice at the time. Most interestingly perhaps is the allowance of being transposed into different geographies, histories demographics. Feeling out of water has its silver lining.

In what ways do you believe that the medium of 16mm film allows for a unique expression of narrative compared to digital formats?

You're forced to deal with the tactile qualities of 16mm—its format forces a recognition of linearity that will either be embraced or reconstituted. Regardless, time is conditional and images are made further concrete. There's too much liquidity in digital formats. I value them for what they are but the advantage of 16mm are its limits and contending with what you've captured in its footage, for better or worse.

As the founder of Galería Perdida, how has your involvement in collective spaces shaped your perspective on collaboration and community in the arts?

Galería Perdida recognized collectivity as a persuasive argument against the character of the singular artist and the character of the exhibiting institution. Collaboration was necessary for its success but not inherently the only manner of production. That is, the name was driving force to foment context around a work of art. How does a gallery become responsible for the production of the artwork and not only its exhibition? It's a conflict of interest surely, but a confounding and confusing enterprise. One that suggests that collaboration is best steered under a homogenized identity and community a novelty of better times.

Matt Gondek on Art, Icons Anarchy

The artist reveals his DIY journey and punk rock influences

***Matt Gondek's** visionary Deconstructive Pop Art boldly disrupts iconic imagery, combining playfulness with a punk spirit to redefine pop culture's symbols.*

His art merges vibrant colors with deconstructed icons, embodying rebellion and critique. In this interview, he discusses punk roots, art business challenges balancing approachability with dark themes of anarchy and pessimism.

Matt Gondek, an innovator in Deconstructive Pop Art, has established himself as a defining voice in contemporary art, reshaping the way we interpret icons of pop culture. Known for his audacious style and unapologetic dismantling of familiar cartoon heroes, Gondek's work pairs a vivid, punchy color palette with a punk ethos that celebrates rebellion and critiques the allure of mainstream idols. His art, a fusion of high-energy destruction and nostalgia, is both a tribute and a deconstruction of modern mythologies, challenging viewers to reconsider the value we place on cultural icons. Gondek's pieces have captivated audiences worldwide, leading to sold-out exhibitions in cultural hubs like Los Angeles, New York, Paris beyond.

In this interview, Gondek opens up about his DIY beginnings, the inspirations drawn from childhood heroes his unapologetic approach to the art business. Gondek reveals what it means to be a self-made artist in a world of gatekeepers, explaining how he balances the practicalities of the art industry with a raw, unfiltered creative voice.

How do you define "Deconstructive Pop Art," and what elements do you believe are essential to this style in your work?

I spent a lot of time in punk bands I learned about DIY ethics. I've always leaned that way – I question authority and tear down hierarchy, so that's where the deconstruction part comes from. The icons come from my childhood heroes like Mickey Mouse and Bart Simpson. I tear down these icons through my work, so that's deconstructive pop art.

Can you share the inspiration behind your unique approach to deconstructing cartoon icons and pop culture figures?

There's been a few. Andy Warhol, who's from Pittsburgh, like me. He didn't influence me in the sense that our styles are the same, but he influenced me in terms of the networking and business side of the artwork and his business acumen.

Also Roy Lichtenstein and his Ben-Day dots were a key influence. Lichtenstein is my favourite artist I like how he took comic books and cartoons and turned them into fine art using the same printing methods – it's fascinating.

Your work features a vibrant colour palette and playful tone. How do these choices reflect your message or critique of societal norms?

I use bright and poppy colours because it makes the work more approachable and digestible. By painting things bright and fun, I'm able to reach a wider audience while still dealing with things like pessimism, addiction, anarchy, etc.

What role does your punk rock spirit play in your artistic process and the themes you explore in your work?

The biggest takeaway from punk rock is the Do-It-Yourself mentality. When I began as an artist I put on my own shows, made my own clothes and prints, etc. Now, the anti-authority and self betterment side of Punk comes through more in the work.

As a self-taught artist, what challenges have you faced in developing your voice how have you overcome them?

The higher up the ladder you go in the art world, the more doors are in your way - and it really is all about who you know.

The biggest challenge I faced starting out was that I didn't know anyone.

Through your podcast, Clean Break, you discuss the business aspects of creativity. How do you balance the commercial side of art with your artistic integrity?

I don't balance them - because I've always been of the mindset that I make artwork to sustain myself. I think most artists WANT to quit their jobs and solely support themselves off of their art, but they don't know how - or are to afraid to make the changes to do it. That's what the podcast is about - how to make those changes.

Available in

PRINT

Americas to Australia

Europe to Africa Reader's House is available over 190 countries and thousands of retaiers, platforms including Amazon, Barnes & Noble, Walmart, Waterstone's .....

ELECTRONIC

It is an electronic (flip book) format and interactive. Accessable from electronic devices like pc, smart phone, notepads..

ONLINE

All interviews, we conduct make them accessable online for free.

SOCIAL MEDIA

We are on Facebook, Instagram and X. Please follow us on social media @readershousemag

contact us today for an interview opportunity at editor@readershouse.co.uk

Subscribe Now!

YES! I would like a subscription to

☐ Current Issue for ☐ Includes Shipping and Handling

☐ One-Year Subscription (_____ Issues) for

☐ Two-Year Subscription (_____ Issues) for

☐ I am a renewing a current subscription ☐ I am a new subscriber

Name: ____________________ Phone: ____________

Shipping Address: ____________________

Billing Address: ____________________

Email: ____________________

☐ Yes, I would like to receive updates, newsletters and special offers

☐ No, I would NOT like to receive updates, newsletters and special offers

Payment Type: ☐ Cash ☐ Check

Please mail this form to:
Magazine Name: *Reader's House* by Newyox 200 Suite, 134-146 Curtain Road EC2A 3AR London readershouse.co.uk

www.ingramcontent.com/pod-product-compliance
Lightning Source LLC
Chambersburg PA
CBHW041206100726
47911CB00016B/873
9781642264470